Growing Up
BLACK

Teens Write About
African-American Identity

By Youth Communication

Edited by Maria Luisa Tucker

YOUTH
COMMUNICATION
True Stories by Teens

Growing Up BLACK

EXECUTIVE EDITORS
Keith Hefner and Laura Longhine

CONTRIBUTING EDITORS
Nora McCarthy, Hope Vanderberg, Rachel Blustain,
Tamar Rothenberg, Andrea Estepa, Katia Hetter, Philip
Kay, Al Desetta, Clarence Haynes, and Autumn Spanne

LAYOUT & DESIGN
Efrain Reyes, Jr. and Jeff Faerber

PRODUCTION
Stephanie Liu

COVER ART
YC Art Dept.

For reprint information, please contact Youth Communication.

ISBN 978-1-935552-34-5

Second, Expanded Edition

Printed in the United States of America

Youth Communication ®
New York, New York
www.youthcomm.org

Catalog Item #YD07-1

Table of Contents

How the Other Half Lives

Natasha Santos 15

> Natasha interviews minority teens in the suburbs to
> explore the relationship between race and success.

Not Black Enough?

Jamal Greene 21

> Jamal speaks standard English, can't dance, and prefers
> baseball to basketball. Does this mean he's less black
> than his peers?

I'm Black, He's Puerto Rican. So What?

Artiqua Steed 26

> Artiqua, who's black, is pressured to break off her
> relationship with Johnny, a Puerto Rican.

Shopping While Black

Stephanie Hinkson 30

> Stephanie resents being followed in stores because she's
> young, black, and stereotyped as a shoplifter.

Rappin' with the 5-0

Allen Francis 34

> Allen visits a police precinct to see what cops are really
> like.

Contents

Princess Oreo Speaks Out

Dwan "Telly" Carter 38
>   Dwan is teased by fellow blacks for "acting white" and
>   wonders why people can't be more open-minded.

Lightening My Skin, Straightening My Hair

Samantha Brown 43
>   Samantha tries to change her appearance after noticing
>   that the few black models in teen magazines tend to be
>   light-skinned with long, soft hair.

The Whitest Black Girl

Nicole Hawkins..46
>   As a biracial child, Nicole gets teased by those who
>   can't fit her into a category.

Barack Is Black

April Daley 51
>   Like Barack Obama, April has been wrongly accused of
>   not being "black enough."

Barack Is Black...But Not African-American

Donald Moore 55
>   By Donald's definition, Barack Obama is not African-
>   American, because he doesn't share the history and
>   experience of most blacks in the U.S.

Contents

Don't Follow the Leader

Anonymous.. 60

> *The author wonders how much your surroundings*
> *influence your goals in life.*

Big, Black, and Beautiful

Anonymous.. 65

> *As a black girl attending a mostly white school, the*
> *writer gets the message that only thin, blond girls are*
> *considered appealing, and she is not one of them.*

The N-Word

Desiree Bailey.. 69

> *Desiree is not buying the argument that blacks can use*
> *the "n-word" in an empowering or affectionate way.*

Singled Out

Angelina Darrisaw 73

> *Angelina feels out of place at the elite private school she*
> *attends where she's one of the only black students.*

The Flag's Not for Me

Anonymous.. 79

> *The writer is angry about the gap between American*
> *ideals of liberty and justice for all and the reality of*
> *discrimination and injustice.*

Where My Girls At?

Danielle Chambers 83

> Danielle is disgusted by the ways mainstream hip-hop
> disrespects women, and argues that it damages the
> entire black community.

My First White Friend

Anita Ames 88

> When Anita befriends Meghan, the only white girl in
> her grade, she learns about a culture she never
> experienced before.

Black Girl, White Campus

Samantha Brown 91

> Samantha, who is black, has a difficult adjustment to
> an overwhelmingly white college.

Coloring Outside the Lines

Desiree Bailey 93

> When she enters the 7th grade as the only black student
> in her class, Desiree is thrown into confusion about her
> racial identity.

Black Pride, and a New Ride

Norman Brant 100

> Norman wants the finer things in life, and he wants to
> get them through hard work and education, not by
> selling drugs.

Contents

A Floor for Every Race

April Daley 104

> At April's school, students segregate themselves by
> hanging out in different hallways according to race and
> ethnicity.

Racism Ended Our Relationship

Lenny Jones 107

> Lenny feels conflicted about dating a white girl.

All Mixed Up

Satra Wasserman 113

> As the son of a black mother and white Jewish father,
> Satra doesn't fit into society's categories and gets
> teased and rejected.

FICTION SPECIAL: Lost and Found

Anne Schraff 118

Using the Book

Teens: How to Get More Out of This Book........................128

How to Use This Book in Staff Training.............................129

Teachers & Staff: How to Use This Book in Groups.........130

Credits.. 132

About Youth Communication 133

About the Editors.. 136

More Helpful Books from Youth Communication 138

Introduction

How much does the color of your skin shape you? What does it mean to "act black"? And what is "race," anyway?

In their search for answers to these questions, the African-American teens in this book explore a wide-ranging world of black experience, from a Brooklyn ghetto to the tea house of a mostly white prep school. In each story, the authors unflinchingly confront the problem of race; they reveal their insecurities about being "too black" or "not black enough," bump up against their own prejudices, and express anger when they encounter racism.

"I'm still confused about what it means to be black," writes Jamal. He tries to define "race" but finds that there are competing understandings of it—one definition says it's genetic, the other says it's about a shared attitude and culture. The definition of race comes up again in two dueling essays about whether President Barack Obama is "black enough" to be considered African-American, since his mother was white and his father was Kenyan.

Several authors describe the tension between fitting in with white culture and being "true" to their race. After years of relaxing her hair and trying to lighten her skin, Samantha gets fed up and gives up her beauty routine. "I just couldn't bother with all the aggravation it took to try to be someone that I knew I wasn't and could never be," she writes, vowing not to read another teen magazine until she can open it up "and see a dark-skinned girl with her hair in dreads or just natural, with her 10 dark-skinned friends standing next to her."

Our authors feel their skin color most intensely when they're the only black kids around. As students in mostly white schools, the authors of "A Floor for Every Race" and "Singled Out" feel awkward and out of place at first, but find comfort when they form friendships with the few other black students. April explains that the black students congregate on the 5th floor and the Asian kids have the 6th floor, but that, "We don't use the floors as our separate victory corners where we chant one race's superiority over another. They are simply small communities."

However, where some writers find that shared skin color helps them connect with fellow African-Americans, others just feel constrained by it. In "Princess Oreo Speaks Out," both friends and family tease Dwan because she likes rock music and doesn't use slang. Biracial authors Nicole and Satra are also teased because they don't quite fit in with either of their cultures, but they resist pressure to pick sides. "The biggest favor I did for myself was not trying to choose one race to be," writes Satra.

Several writers describe the sting of racism. In "Shopping While Black," Stephanie confronts a store worker who assumes she's a shoplifter. In "The Flag's Not For Me," the anonymous author explains how he lost his childhood patriotism when he learned about cases of police brutality. "The American flag has been used as a mask to hide the true face of America, a face covered with blemishes of discrimination," he writes.

Other stories tackle the rocky terrain of interracial dating and friendships, resentment toward African-Americans who are financially better off, and the obstacles particular to young black men growing up in the 'hood. Interspersed among these powerful personal narratives are reported pieces that analyze specific aspects of the black experience: the history of the N-word, the economics of drug dealing, the troubled relationship between cops and black teens.

Although the authors here may share a common label, these stories are not just for African-American readers. We hope teens of all races and ethnicities will recognize some of the voices on these pages, and that the stories will help them explore their own ideas about race.

In the following stories, names have been changed: *I'm Black, He's Puerto Rican. So What?*, *The N-Word*, and *Coloring Outside the Lines*.

Ruda Tillett

How the Other Half Lives

By Natasha Santos

For a long time I believed that roaches, violence, and chaos were part of everyone's childhood memories. In my neighborhood, Brownsville, Brooklyn, poor blacks and Latinos live isolated from wealthier minorities and other races. I've often been afraid to walk down my block alone for fear of being attacked.

As I got older, I realized that other people weren't living in fear like I was. I began to feel like a statistic—a black girl who lived in a place where mothers dote on drug-dealing sons and ignore the gun hidden under dirty laundry in the closet. I wondered if I had less of a chance to achieve the American dream because I had had less of a childhood. I wondered whether my race and the poverty I grew up in would hold me back from success and happiness. I had guidance counselors and teachers who sang the same old song about reaching for the stars and being determined, and I bought it enough to get good grades and plan to go to college. But those dreams were starting to sound like fairy tales.

I wanted to interview other teens to find out how they thought their neighborhood, race, and class might affect their lives. The editor at my after-school journalism program told me that she had been brought up in a suburban town where many races and classes attended the same school peacefully. I wanted to visit this place, partly see how the other half lived (the wealthy, suburban, BMW-driving, as-seen-on-TV people) and partly to prove my editor wrong. The idea that many races and classes could live together in a kind of unified community seemed unreal to me.

Growing up, I'd been taught that most black people live in poor neighborhoods in cities, while the suburban life is a kind of Caucasian paradise. Even though I attend a racially and eco-nomically diverse high school in New York City, I just couldn't picture a school in the suburbs looking like mine.

The idea that many races and classes could live together in a kind of unified community seemed unreal to me.

I brought all my skepti-cism with me the morning we got off the train in Norwalk, Connecticut, expecting the cliché of private houses owned by scared upper-class Caucasians ready to move out as soon as a family of color moved in. Indeed, much of Norwalk looked the way I expected. I saw neatly manicured lawns with houses tucked serenely into foliage and generously spaced apart, giving the inhabitants enough room to have a 50-person cookout in the backyard without disturbing their neighbors.

When we arrived at Brien McMahon, my editor's old high school, I noticed it had a parking lot. "That says it all," I thought. A vision of Beverly Hills 90210 came to me: all the students driv-ing to school in their Ferraris and BMWs with surfers' bodies and manicured nails.

So walking inside, I was surprised to find a setting resembling my school: Diversity, loudness, cliques, and teachers in the halls making sure that everyone was in line. This was disappointing. For the story I planned to write, I was counting on the school to serve as a metaphor for how naive and sheltered these suburban teens were.

I sat down at a table in the cafeteria to question seven teens who had agreed to be interviewed. Jesse, Amanda, Dipti, Daphney, Ashiah, Jessica, and Malcolm openly answered the questions we threw at them. Three were black, one was half-black/half-white, one was Asian-American, one was half-Cuban/half-white, and one was Indian-American. When we asked them how they believed their race and class might affect their lives, their answers surprised me. Though they were from different countries, different classes, and of different races, they all agreed that African-Americans and other minorities are poor more because of their mindset than because of race.

Daphney, who is black and whose family came from Haiti, said black kids at that school hold themselves back more than the system does. "I think it's because they have fallen into their own stereotypes. They criticize the people who want to get ahead," Daphney said. "This kid asked my sister, 'How come you get such good grades? Black people aren't supposed to get such good grades.'"

Daphney's dad is a realtor and her mom is a nurse's aide. They moved to Norwalk because they wanted to raise her in a mixed environment, not just among Haitian- and African-Americans. Daphney said her family is just the opposite of African-Americans who don't believe blacks can make it. They constantly push her to do well in school. "I'll be the first generation in my family to go to college and I feel pressure... [my parents say], 'Why can't you get a 4.0 in high school?'" Daphney told us.

Ashiah, who is black and Haitian as well, said she also believes that African-Americans are their own downfall. "I think black people are stuck in the past. White people beat the blacks in the past so now I hear people saying, 'Master beat me so now I can't get up in the morning.' It's a joke but they're serious. I don't think white people have anything to do with it."

Ashiah said she's also under constant pressure to perform in school. Dipti, who came to the U.S. from India at age 2, said she felt the same way. Most of her adult relatives are professionals in high-demand fields such as engineering and medicine, and Dipti said she dreams of going into medicine, too. She had her entire college and professional career planned out.

Jessica, whose mom is black and dad is white, was the only one in the group who said she'd had a direct experience with racism. Although Jessica now lives in one of the wealthiest communities in Norwalk, she said her mom had been a target of racism in the past and had faced discrimination from blacks and whites when she married a white man. Even so, Jessica agreed with the others that your life is shaped mostly by what you do for yourself and the only person holding someone back is herself.

Instead of finding their ideas about race liberating or hopeful, I simply thought, "These kids are obviously naïve. They haven't been crowded into understaffed, segregated schools. They haven't been afraid to walk down their blocks alone. They haven't lived." I guess my feelings were obvious, since I sat there looking a bit surly and most of the kids seemed to avoid eye contact with me.

Visiting Norwalk brought me back to another time in my life when I felt angry and different from my classmates. In the beginning of elementary school, my best friend was a quiet girl of Middle Eastern descent named Farrah. Like most of my first grade classmates, she lived on the "other side" of the school, the "good" side. The school was a border between the poor side of the neighborhood, where I lived, and the well off who lived in comfy houses. I never visited Farrah's house. She never invited me. Maybe in our own ways we could both sense my jealousy.

Farrah and the kids from the "other side" seemed well kept and happy. Farrah told me her dad drove a cab and her mother always fixed her a snack when she came home. My dad was in jail or never around. When I came home from school, my mom was usually in her bed watching TV or sleeping.

I was unhappy, unkempt, and malnourished. I felt like an outcast among the perfectly clean, perfectly white 6-year-old kids with parents who noticed every skinned knee and missing tooth. My mother didn't know my birthday, much less if I had a skinned knee.

The suburban teens agreed that African-Americans are poor more because of their mindset than because of race.

My jealousy turned into anger and anger turned into violence. I took out my anger about my family and the unfairness of life on Farrah. I stole her things, pulled her hair, and tried to stab her with a pencil once. I picked on her because her family represented, for me, the normality that I wished my family had.

Visiting those teens in Norwalk reminded me once again of all the advantages I haven't had in life and made me feel doomed to fall through the cracks in society. In the months after the interview, I wrote several angry drafts of this story, lashing out at those teens for living in a bubble. I just wanted to rant about all the experiences I could've had, all the things I could've been if I had been born into their lives. I felt frustrated and shortchanged. What invisible hand had given me hamburger while they got steak? Why them and not me?

But as time passed, I started to feel a bit ashamed of the things I said in my rants—the stereotypes I was writing about rich people and white people, even though most of the teens we met in Norwalk weren't rich or white, just working- and middle-class. It took me a year to sort out all my feelings and think through what they were saying.

I still think those teens are naïve to believe that race hasn't and won't shape their lives in any way, but at the same time I could kind of see why they would think that way. They've been lucky enough to live in a place where racial and social boundaries don't seem as constricting as they feel to me, living in Brownsville.

These days I'm feeling a bit more hopeful that success comes from a mixture of things—not just where you come from and how society views you, but also what you think and who you are and how much you work for it. There are those who escape the mold and go on to be great despite their background and culture. They are the exceptions, but I'm trying to believe I'm capable of being one of them.

Maybe one day—when I've gone to college and have a six-figure salary—I can shed my jealousy and pessimism. Maybe I'll move from Brownsville and find a place in the surreal suburbs. Maybe one day it'll be my kids who are saying that success has nothing to do with race, that those days are over and that it's all in my head. Maybe.

Natasha was 17 when she wrote this story. She graduated from high school, worked as an Americorps volunteer in New Orleans, and went to college.

YC Art Dept.

Not Black Enough?

By Jamal Greene

I am black. Yet, since I was 12 I've gone to a school almost totally devoid of black people. I don't speak in slang. I don't listen to rap or reggae and, try as I might, I have at best a 50-50 chance of converting a lay-up. Except for the fact that I'm not white, I am not all that different from a stereotypical white kid from Queens, New York.

Because of this, when I am around other black people, I usually feel a certain distance between us. And so do they. For example, this past summer I took a journalism workshop at New York University. After it was over, I was on the phone with one of the girls in the workshop, a black girl, and we got to talking about first impressions. She said that for about the first week of the workshop, she was saying to herself, "What's wrong with this guy? Is he white or something?" She said that I talked like a "cracker" (as she put it) and she made a lot of offhand remarks about me not being a "real" black person. It irritated me that this girl thought that just because I didn't speak Black English, I was not a genuine black person.

I have often heard people criticize Yankee announcer Paul Olden for the same thing. Olden is black, but you would never know it from the way he talks. They say he's trying to be white. I don't "sound black" either and I'm not trying to be anything but who I am. It's just the way I talk. Black people who speak standard English don't do it because they want to dissociate themselves from other black people but because they grew up hearing English spoken that way.

Just look at the English boxer Lennox Lewis. He's black but his accent is as British as can be. Is he "trying to be English" and denying his black roots? Of course not. He just grew up around people who had British accents.

She said that I talked like a "cracker" and made a lot of offhand remarks about me not being a "real" black person.

I don't dance like a lot of other black people either. I never learned to move my hips and legs the way most kids you see at parties are able to. I lose the beat if I have to move more than two body parts at once and so my dancing tends to get a little repetitive. When I go to parties with black people I often find myself sitting at the table drinking a Coke while everybody else is dancing. "Why aren't you dancing?" people ask. And then when I do get on the dance floor, the same people sneer at me. "What's wrong with you?" they say. "Why do you just keep doing the same thing over and over again?"

Contrary to popular belief, black people aren't born with the ability to dance and play basketball. Even though I have speed and leaping ability, I can't drive to the hole without losing my dribble. Those skills have to be learned and perfected with experience. It only seems like they are innate because the black community in America is culturally very close-knit and people share the same interests.

Another thing that constitutes "blackness" in a lot of people's minds is an interest in or a feeling of pride and identification with things historically black. I collected baseball cards until I was 15. I had a pretty substantial collection for a kid. At least, I thought I did. One afternoon, my cousins came over to my house and were looking at my baseball cards.

"Do you have any Jackie Robinson cards?" one of them asked.

"Of course not," I answered.

They were visibly displeased with that response. Of course, in my mind I knew that the reason I didn't have any Jackie Robinson cards was the same reason I didn't have any Ted Williams or Mickey Mantle or Joe Dimaggio cards: I just didn't have the money for legendary players. Even if I were going to spend that money on baseball cards, I would buy a Mickey Mantle card before I would buy a Jackie Robinson card of the same price; Jackie may have been the first black major leaguer, but Mickey hit home runs and home runs increase in value faster than historical novelty. It's that simple. But my cousins thought that the reason I didn't have any Jackie Robinson cards was because I didn't like black players as much as white players.

My family has always had a problem with me liking baseball—a game that did not integrate until 1947—as much as I do. They keep getting me these Negro League postcards because they are worried that I don't know enough about the subject. And they're right. But then again, sports enthusiasts in general don't know enough about the Negro Leagues. My family feels very strongly that as a black sports fan, I should feel an added responsibility to know about black baseball players. If I don't learn about them, they say, then nobody will.

Minorities are often called upon to be the spokespeople for their races. The only black kid in the class is almost always asked to speak when the subjects of slavery or the civil rights movement come up. The question is, does he have a responsibility to know more about issues pertaining to blacks than his white classmates? I would like to think that he doesn't.

If we really believe that everyone should be treated equally, then ideally my Jewish friends should be expected to know just as much about black history as I do. Of course I should know more about the Negro Leagues than I do now, but so should a white baseball fan or a Japanese baseball fan or a polka-dot baseball fan.

So I guess I don't fit in with the black people who speak Black English, dance with a lot of hip motion, and hang out with an all-black crowd. And I don't feel any added responsibility to learn about black history or go out and associate with more black people, either. Nor do I fit in with blacks who try as hard as they can to separate themselves from blacks altogether, vote Republican, and marry white women. I don't do that, either.

Even though I grew up playing Wiffle Ball with white kids in Park Slope instead of basketball with black kids in Bed Stuy, even though I go to a school with very few blacks, and even though most of my friends are white and Asian, I can't say that I feel completely at home with white people either. Achieving racial equality is a process that still has a long way to go. Blacks were slaves just 150 years ago. Until just 45 years ago, we were legally inferior to whites. Blacks may have achieved equality before the law, but it will take another few generations to achieve social equality.

There is still a stigma attached to interracial relationships, for example, both romantic and otherwise. Whenever I'm around the parents of white friends, I get the sense that they see me not as "that nice kid who is friends with my son or daughter" but rather as "that nice black kid who is friends with my son or daughter." There is still a line that certain people are unwilling to cross.

So after all this analysis, I'm still confused about what it means to be black. What is race, anyway? According to Webster's, race is "a class or kind of people unified by a community of interests, habits, or characteristics." Well, anyone who's ever called me or any other black person "white on the inside" because we didn't fit their stereotype can look at that definition and claim victory. "There it is, right in the dictionary," they're saying, "black is an attitude, not just a color."

By that definition I'm not black at all. But I was black the last time I looked in the mirror. So I went back to the dictionary and found that Webster's has another definition for race: "a division of mankind possessing traits that are transmissible by descent and sufficient to characterize it as a distinct human type."

I'm still confused about what it means to be black. What is race, anyway?

Wait a minute! Does that mean that a black person is anyone with dark skin, full lips, a broad nose, and coarse hair? These are traits transmissible by descent and distinct to black people. By the second definition, to be black means to have these physical characteristics. Speaking Black English and dancing well are not genetic. They are cultural and arise from blacks living isolated from other communities.

Which definition is right? I would like to think that it is the second. I would like to think that race is nothing more than the color of your skin, but clearly in most people's minds it's more than that. I feel distanced from blacks because I am black but don't act the part, and I feel distanced from whites because I act white but don't look the part. As long as other people expect me to act a certain way because of the way I look, or to look a certain way because of the way I act, I will continue to be something of an outcast because I defy their prejudices.

Society has different expectations of blacks and whites, and becomes uncomfortable if any of us stray from those expectations. Just ask anybody who's ever picked me for two-on-two just because I was black.

Jamal wrote this story when he was 16. After high school and college, he worked as a sports journalist, went to Yale Law School, and became a law professor.

Jose Rodriguez

I'm Black, He's Puerto Rican. So What?

By Artiqua Steed

One day I was walking down the street with my best friend and my sister when this guy rode by us on a bike. I noticed him right away. He had a caramel-colored complexion and very pretty eyes, kind of like my father.

I told my friend that I thought he was cute. So she turned around and called him. "Hey, hey you, on the bike," she said. He turned around. "Yeah, you, come here," she said. "My friend wants to talk to you."

I was very embarrassed. I couldn't believe she had actually done that. But it worked. The guy started to come back toward us. I had thought he was a light-skinned black, but I saw as he came closer that he was Latino. I thought to myself, "It must be really dark out here for me not to have noticed before that he's

Puerto Rican." But since he was cute I didn't really care.

I was very nervous. I didn't even ask him his name. All I could say was hi. He asked me my name and how old I was. We talked for a few minutes and then he asked me for my number. I didn't want to give it to a guy I didn't know, but I took his. When he gave me the paper I looked down at it and it said Johnny. "Johnny," I thought, "What kind of name is that?" It was so plain. I'm used to unusual names. Besides, I thought he would have a Hispanic name.

He told me to call him the next day at 3 p.m. After I walked away from him I had a huge grin on my face. When I finally caught up to my sister and my friend, they started laughing at me. But I didn't mind.

I called Johnny the next day at around 3, like he asked. The phone rang and then a recording came on. I was mad. How could he tell me to call and then not be there? I called him back about 20 minutes later. This time he answered. We talked for two hours about everything. He told me about himself and the things he liked to do. He told me that he was a DJ and also wrote songs.

When I called Johnny, my brother would say things like, "Are you on the phone with that rice-and-bean-eating Puerto Rican?"

After three days of talking on the phone, we finally decided to see each other again. We had a nice time even though we only went to his house. He made a compilation of all of my favorite songs. We spoke to each other every day after that. After three or four weeks, he asked me to go out with him. I said yes before he could finish his sentence.

I didn't know what I was getting myself into—him being Puerto Rican and me being black. I'd never had an interracial relationship before, and it caught me by surprise. I'd thought about the issue of dating someone of another race, but could never imagine myself doing it. I was always very into black pride and thought that any black man who thought another woman was more beautiful than a black woman was crazy. And I strongly believed that a black woman who dated a man of another race was ignoring how hard black men had to work to get where they are.

But when I met Johnny my attitude started to change. I still have pride in my race, but I came to realize that if a black woman dates a man of another race, it doesn't mean that she's given up on black men. And thinking that black women are more beautiful than women of any other race is just going overboard.

I have to admit that the fact that Johnny is not black is one of the reasons why I started liking him so much. I thought it would be different to date someone who was not black. I was excited to learn more about him and his background, culture, and beliefs. I wanted to see the world from his perspective. I even found myself trying to learn Spanish.

My brother and sister and even some of my friends gave me a hard time for going out with Johnny. When I called him, my brother would say things like, "Are you on the phone with that rice-and-bean-eating Puerto Rican?"

My sister was even worse. She is what you would call a bigot. She feels that there is no need for anyone in her family to be dating someone who is not black. My best friend once asked my sister, "What would you do if I married a white man?" My sister's exact words were, "Don't bring him to my house." She once told me that she didn't like Johnny and I know it's because he's not black.

I have to admit that when Johnny and I first started going out, it was hard for me to get past my own stereotypes about Puerto Ricans. I thought they had no color coordination (my sister always said that they were the ones who came outside with mismatched colors and no socks), that all they liked to eat was rice and beans, and that they were always copying black fashions and music.

Before meeting Johnny, I often found myself in conversations that were critical of Latinos. I remember one time when my sister and I saw a Puerto Rican couple fighting on the street. The guy was hitting the girl. I said to my sister that if the girl had been black, she would have fought back. My sister agreed with me. I never considered that the girl was just scared of her boyfriend.

Now when I hear racial slurs against Puerto Ricans, I am offended by them, because I've learned that they are not true. It hurts me when people dis Puerto Ricans because they are talking about my boyfriend. Whenever my friends and family do it, it makes me feel bad because they don't see that they are talking about someone I care a lot about. The other day, I snapped at my sister for saying something stupid about Puerto Ricans.

At first, it was hard to look at him and not see his color.

As far as I know, Johnny's family has never said anything against me or our relationship. Some of his friends even told him they thought I was pretty and asked him if I had any friends for them. He does have one friend who doesn't like morenas (a Spanish name for dark-skinned girls), but I've never met the guy and he hasn't done anything to come between us.

Johnny and I have been going out for several months now and we get along fine considering the racial difference. I feel that he respects me more than any other guy I have dated. This doesn't have anything to do with the fact that he is not black; it's just the type of person he is. The hard part is dealing with other people's attitudes. Interracial dating is still hard for a lot of folks to accept. But if two people are in love or like each other a lot, then racial or ethnic differences will not wreck the relationship.

The author was 15 when she wrote this story.

YC Art Dept.

Shopping While Black

By Stephanie Hinkson

"Excuse me, miss, do you need help?"

"No, thank you. I do not."

That's how it often starts. She asks me if I need help and pretends to fix something. I move, she moves. I stop, she stops. I turn around, she watches. You should be seeing the pattern by now.

I am in a store shopping. I am African-American and young, and I think it's because of my race and age that she, the store employee, thinks I'm going to steal. What's funny is that the employees are of all races. Yes, the black and Hispanic ones are on my back also.

It usually takes them less than two minutes after I walk into the store to get within a few feet of me. Their faulty radar turns their eyes laser-beam red and they fly over to me, pretending to fix the shirts on the rack or the pants on the shelf behind me.

It really hits me that they're watching me like a surveillance camera when I'm focused on the clothes I'm about to buy and realize they haven't moved. If I'm looking at something for two minutes and you are still straightening the clothes next to me, there's definitely a problem.

This is when I get angry. It's not the Jim Crow era any more, but I feel like people still can't get past the color of my skin. Yes, I am young, I am black, and I want something from your store. But I am not going to steal it and I feel angry that anyone would suspect me of doing so. I don't think I look suspicious. I'm quiet and I dress nicely; I usually wear high heels and dressy shirts and I carry myself maturely.

I wouldn't shoplift because my mother taught me better than that. I'm a Christian and I believe that stealing is wrong. Plus, it's a crime and I'd never do anything to jeopardize my future. So if someone assumes differently, I feel offended. They don't understand who I am.

Yes, I am young, I am black, and I want something from your store. But I'm not going to steal.

I first try to ignore the "red eye" so I can keep my cool and continue looking at the clothes. Sometimes she's still right behind me. That's when my question comes out.

"Is there a problem?" I ask the red eye.

"Problem? There's no problem," is the usual reply.

"Well, I think there is because you have been following me since I came into the store and I didn't ask for any help, so can you please excuse me?" I've said this more times than I can remember.

Sometimes they'll apologize and try to appear sorry. Other times they glare at me like they want to take it outside. Whenever that happens I let them know, "If there is a problem I can always go speak to your manager." That's when they back off.

One day I went shopping with my friend Tiffany, who's also African-American. We went into a shoe store, where there were other customers shopping. As we made our way up one aisle, there was the red eye. We went down the aisle—so did the red eye. By the next aisle I knew what was going to happen.

"Tiffy, let's leave, 'cause we are being followed," I told my friend.

"Yeah, for real," Tiffany replied.

Some people ask if being suspected of shoplifting is a race issue or an age issue for me, and I think it's both. When I asked my mother and a couple of other adults of color if they feel like they get followed in stores, their answer was, "Hardly ever." Yes, it might happen occasionally, but not the way it happens to me.

To be fair, I do know teens who steal. Sometimes teenagers shoplift to impress their friends, or to fit in by doing whatever their friends are doing. Some teenagers steal because they have no money and they don't want to be teased for not having the newest name-brand clothes. I've also seen people selling their shoplifted goods on the street to make money.

However, I don't think I'm followed just because I'm young. Another teen I know, Anna, who's white, said she's seldom been followed in stores. And she told me about an incident she saw at the mall.

"I saw two female friends together," Anna said. One was black and one was white. "As I was looking at them," Anna continued, "the white girl took something." One of the store clerks suspected something and walked up to the two of them, but approached the black girl, and the white girl walked out of the store. "The true culprit got off," Anna said.

The friends were both young, but the black girl got singled out most likely because of her race. Anna's story upset me but it didn't surprise me. There have been many times when I've been in a store and white people weren't followed but I was.

Many adults of color report discrimination in stores, too. In one Gallup poll, almost a third of the black adults surveyed said that in the previous month, they'd been treated unfairly in a store because they were black.

I understand that shoplifting is a problem. Stores lose out when people steal. An annual survey of stores estimates that nationwide there are about a million shoplifting incidents every day, totaling a loss of around $10 billion a year. But store management's acting as if only certain races steal doesn't benefit them. In 2002, Sharon Simmons-Thomas, an African-American secretary, sued Macy's for racial profiling. She said that though innocent of shoplifting, she was detained and mistreated by Macy's security personnel because of her race.

"Is there a problem?" I ask the red eye.

Macy's paid to settle the case in 2004, so it didn't go to trial. In January 2005, Macy's settled another lawsuit over alleged racial profiling of black and Latino customers, brought by New York's Attorney General. Macy's had to pay $600,000 in damages and change its security practices.

Teenagers who feel like they are targets for the red eye don't have to stand there and take it. I've been followed enough times that I've figured out how to deal with it. Sometimes I ask to speak to the manager, which usually results in the employee trying to apologize and keep it hush-hush. Or I'll decide not to spend my money in that particular store and leave. If you trail me like you're a predator hunting your prey, then I do not need to spend my money in your store.

If you're an honest person, you should not be made to feel like a criminal. And if you are a teenage shoplifter, you're making it hard on the rest of us. Shoplifting is a crime and you can go to jail for it. Think twice before you take something. Finally, to all of you red eyes: the next time you see a young person of color in your store, keep in mind that not all minorities steal, and neither do all teens.

Stephanie was 18 when she wrote this story.

Dylan Tucker

Rappin' with the 5-0

By Allen Francis

Before I decided to do this story, I'd never had any dealings with the police and that was OK with me. I had heard too many stories from family and friends about the brutal nature of cops and seen too many examples of it on the news.

It was all too easy for me to imagine being stopped by a cop one day and hearing those deadly words, "You fit the description of..." The scene would end with the cop beating me over the head with his nightstick while humming his favorite song.

I decided I needed to lighten up a bit. Some cops may be brutal or crooked, but not all of them, right? I wanted to find out for myself what cops are really like and experience some of what they have to do on the job. Then I could share whatever I learned with you, the reader. So I set out for my neighborhood precinct, the 42nd, in the Bronx, New York.

As I got ready to leave the house, my mother told me to put a hat on to cover my braids. I usually wear a bandana, but she says it makes me look like a "hoodlum."

My mom was nervous about me entering police territory but I wasn't. All I was going to do was ask to talk to the youth affairs officer about teen programs in the precinct and the tensions that exist between cops and teenagers. No problem.

As I was walking to the precinct, my enthusiasm started to drain out of me. With each step I thought of better things I could be doing—reading a comic, watching TV, sleeping, bungee jumping, lion taming, anything but this.

As I stopped in front of the station house I was glad I had my hat on. I didn't want to be fighting off cops because I fit the description of some guy with braids who had just robbed a bank or something.

I could see it now, one cop in riot gear yelling, "We need backup, there's a black guy on the premises!"

I could see it now, one cop in riot gear yelling, "We need backup, repeat, backup, there's a black guy on the premises!" Swarms of cops busting out of windows and doors, wielding batons that have my name on them, and not a video camera in sight. Man, I really needed to relax.

The first thing I saw when I walked in was a long bench with about four cops sitting on it—just waiting for me. I asked to see the youth affairs officer. They all looked at each other and finally one of them said she was in a conference.

I asked how long she would be busy and was told, "For an hour or two." Oh fiddlesticks, I thought, I wasn't going to get to sit in a police station and interview cops. I was so disappointed, gosh darn the luck.

I wrote out a note asking for an interview. I left my phone number and a copy of the magazine I write for with the officer behind the desk and asked him to make sure the youth officer got it. He said, "Sure," but something about the way he put the message and magazine down gave me the feeling that the youth officer would never see it.

A few days later I was at it again, trying to find the 10th precinct in Manhattan. (I picked it because it was close to my writing internship.) When I saw the cruisers parked out front, I wiped the sweat off my brow and took a couple of breaths.

I walked in and saw another long bench with three officers sitting on it. I twisted my tongue in knots trying to explain that I was a teen reporter and wanted to talk to the youth affairs officer. I was acting all nervous so I tried to cool out. I got into a stance that suggested I felt totally all right standing in a police station, with braids in my hair, wearing an earring and baggy pants.

One of the cops got on the phone for a minute and then gestured for me to go into the room behind him. "Fitzgerald will answer your questions," he said with a smile.

I walked in like a zombie, saying, "Uh, Officer Fitzgerald?" It was a small room with three people in it. Fitzgerald pulled up a chair for me and I sat down, going through my robotic routine of explaining my name and what my business was.

The other cops left the office and Fitzgerald stood up. This guy was big. He closed the door with his nightstick and we were alone in this small room. This was it. I imagined tomorrow's newspaper with the headline, "In Memory of Allen."

Instead of hitting me with the nightstick, Officer Fitzgerald asked me if I was in high school. When I told him I lived in the Bronx, he told me that his father lived there, too—you know, small talk.

As we got into the interview we would crack a joke here and there. It was amazing—I was relaxing in a squadhouse with the 5-0, the fuzz, the boys in blue. Before I left, Fitzgerald gave me his number and said to call him if he could be of any more help.

Before leaving the precinct, I also met Officer Karen Delancey of youth affairs. She was a beautiful young woman (she told me she had been a model before becoming a cop) who sat down and started talking to me about rap. We were actually rapping songs we both knew in the middle of the police station. Then I remembered I had an interview to do.

I asked her about the tensions between teens and cops, and Officer Delancey talked about how some teens have to show off in front of their friends. They do something wrong, she said, and then they can look cool struggling with the cops or saying they got picked on. I thought she made a point there, but it wasn't the whole story. Sure there are problem teens, but there are also problem cops.

I realized that I had been uncomfortable around all cops because of the actions of the ones who think they're above the law, the ones who harass or brutalize citizens. I had gotten the idea that all cops are like the ones in the bad headlines. But my experience at the 10th precinct showed me that not every cop is that way. Some like to joke around, like Officer Fitzgerald; others are beautiful ex-models like Officer Delancey. Eventually I got to do my interview at the 42nd precinct and that went smoothly, too.

It was amazing—I was relaxing in a squad house with the 5-0, the fuzz, the boys in blue.

Before doing this story, my image of a cop was a bad cop, the kind that abuses power. I'd never run into a "good" cop, the kind who stops walking the beat every once in a while to talk to you. But I know now that there are some out there. My uneasiness around cops hasn't gone away, but my general dislike of cops has. Now I might dislike individual cops because of their actions, but I won't let that turn me against all of them.

Allen wrote this story when he was 18.
He went on to a career in higher education.

Carolina Moya

Princess Oreo Speaks Out

By Dwan "Telly" Carter

"You're just weird."

"If I wasn't looking at chu, I'd have thought you was white."

"Say that again, you said that mad white."

I often get comments like that from classmates, friends, and even my family. Sometimes I laugh, but the comments also hurt my feelings. I know they don't mean anything by it, but I don't like that they think I'm so strange.

I'm a dark-skinned female, a descendent of Africans. I grew up in a black family in a largely black neighborhood, and I'm conscious of the disadvantages that have plagued African-Americans for generations. So what's the deal?

It seems that, for a lot of people around me, being black is an attitude. According to my peers, if you're black, you listen to hip-hop, r&b, and reggae. The ability to dance is a given, of course. You eat Caribbean foods and Southern-style cooking, and if you're female, you know about head wraps and weaves.

Anything beyond that and it's like you're from another planet, or at least that's how I feel. I do a lot of things that people around me don't associate with being black. My friends laugh at me because I'd rather listen to Limp Bizkit than Jay-Z. They love to tease me about watching white teen dramas like *90210*. It doesn't seem to matter that I watch black sitcoms, too. Because of my tastes and the way I talk (I use big vocabulary words), people jokingly call me "Oreo": black on the outside, white on the inside.

But to me, being African-American means my skin color shows a history of enslavement and discrimination. Knowing my history and understanding where I come from is very important to me. It's what keeps me grounded and focused on taking advantage of the opportunities that African-Americans fought for. My dad instilled that knowledge and pride in me. As African-Americans, he says, we should remember our debt to those who risked their lives to give us the opportunities we have, particularly education. His understanding of being black has a lot to do with our history and our future.

I'd never get invited to Soul Train, more like Soul-less Train.

For my peers, being black has more to do with fitting into the culture right here and now. They make me feel like I'm not black enough. And they tease me even more when I try to show them that I can be (their version of) black. When I try to be down with the slang and fit in, half the time I end up sounding like a fool.

"A-ight peace yo."

"You's a Doga man."

"Peace out boo-boo."

It just doesn't come out right. The words get all jumbled and tumble out wrong, and my friends look at me as if I've spoken to them in another language. All my efforts end in giggles (I'm laughing at myself right now) or in gut-busting laughter with tears streaming down my friends' faces. My friends tease me even worse when I try to show them that I can dance to reggae, calypso, and hip-hop. It just doesn't work well. I'd never get invited to *Soul Train*, more like Soul-less Train.

It's not just friends who paint me "white." One time, my sister and I were reciting some lyrics from "You're All I Need," by Method Man featuring Mary J. Blige. My sister was reciting the rap lyrics and I was singing the hook. I was trying to be just like Mary—the bounce in her movements, the way she moved her neck, her hand motions, everything.

I was so into the song, I forgot my sister was in the room with me. I thought I was doing well until my sister's hard laughter broke my concentration. She was doubled over with tears streaming out of her eyes. She was laughing so hard she couldn't talk, and her hand was motioning for me to stop. Then through bits of dying laughter she said, "Stop... stop trying to act ghetto, girl, you making my sides hurt." She said I looked like a duck having seizures. Maybe I didn't move right? Since I'm African-American, I should have some rhythm, huh? And I should be able to mimic Mary? I didn't let it show, but it hurt that even my own sister didn't see me as black enough.

What bothers me about being called white—besides the fact that I'm not—is that it seems I must be lacking something and I'm not sure what it is. My friend told me once, "Maybe one day you'll wake up and become Dwanesha." At the time, I was a geeky freshman in high school, insecure about who I was. I wondered if I could transform myself into someone my peers would recognize as a true black girl.

I'd have loved to put on those big hoop earrings I saw my friends wearing. I imagined myself wearing snake-patterned denim outfits, popping my gum, and showing off a nameplate that said "Dwanesha." My hair would be dyed, fried, and laid to the side. And I'd rank on somebody with those fluid motions of the neck and hand that make the "African-American girl" infamous. Sigh. I would've loved it. I just wanted to fit in.

Then reality knocked some sense into me. I didn't have enough attitude to pull that off. And it just wasn't me. Besides, trying to be Dwanesha would've been like acting out a stereotyped role that isn't very flattering.

Now, as I reach my final semester of my senior year, I'm more aware of myself, who I am, and who I want to be: me. Even saying "Dwanesha" makes me feel weird. That's not who I am. Dwan is my name and I'm comfortable with that. Being different makes me unique. I even gave myself a nickname, "Princess Oreo" (though my dad hates it).

They're not used to an African-American girl bobbing her head along to rock and roll music.

I'm getting used to people staring at me when they hear me blasting rock music. I think it makes them feel uncomfortable because they're not used to an African-American girl bobbing her head along to rock and roll music. "Hey," I want to tell them, "music is music." Besides, rock music was developed by black artists like Little Richard and Chuck Berry well before acts like the Beatles came along. And there's a thin line between musical categories nowadays, and a lot of overlap in musical audiences. Plenty of white kids listen to hip-hop. And I know I'm not the only person of color who listens to pop music.

My reading tastes are diverse, too. I like to read books by white authors, such as Isaac Asimov and Tami Hoag, as well as by black authors, like Octavia Butler, Toni Morrison, and Malcolm X. Maybe it's because I read a lot that I talk the way I do. It's not that I'm purposely acting white—it's not even a thought that crosses my mind. I just like what I like, and I don't know why other people can't be more open-minded.

Even though my dad emphasizes the heritage aspect of being African-American, he's not above making the same cultural assumptions as my friends. One evening, as my family and I were sitting around the dinner table, I turned on the radio and started dancing to the song "Pinch Me," by the Canadian rock band The Barenaked Ladies. Everyone stopped eating and gawked at me (I thought they'd be used to me by now), trying to hold back laughter.

But even when the laughter came, I kept on dancing. My dad said, "It's too late for you, girl." I knew he meant I was hopelessly white. I smiled and started to do my lame air guitar. I didn't care what they thought about me. I was happy. And that was my song.

Dwan was 16 when she wrote this story.
She went on to enroll in Spelman College.

YC Art Dept.

Lightening My Skin, Straightening My Hair

By Samantha Brown

When I was 10 years old, I wanted to see everything and be everything. That meant having phat clothing, a great body, a lot of friends, and a fine cutie on one arm.

I used to collect teen magazines and sit for hours at night reading their quizzes and hair-care tips, and envying the models. These girls seemed too perfect to be true. Every one of my friends wanted to be like them. While we still wore our hair in four, they were already primping and perming. While we were still playing with Ken and Barbie, they were wearing bras, having serious relationships, and battling the problems of sex.

My addiction to teen magazines didn't reach its full height until I entered junior high. I looked to them to help me get a man, learn how to kiss, and master the rules of dating. I believed if I got the proper training from these magazines, I would be set for life.

Most of this time, it didn't really bother me that the teen models were mostly white, or that the black teens who did appear tended to be light-skinned with long, soft, curly hair. This didn't faze my friends, either. We just accepted it as if it were normal. One of my friends even said she hoped to marry a white guy so that her children would have pretty hair. Another friend would go around bragging that she was light-skinned and if anyone had anything to say about it, then they were just jealous.

I wanted to be accepted, and I thought I would be if I had lighter skin and straighter hair, like most of the black models in the teen magazines that we looked to as the ideal of black beauty. So I began a beauty routine to lighten my complexion and straighten my hair. I used skin cream to make my complexion lighter. I would buy 16-ounce bottles for about $4 a piece and plaster it all over my face every night. For a while this strategy appeared to be working—my complexion was a little lighter and people even commented on it. But when I ran out of money, I also ran out of skin cream.

Then I began begging my mother to let me get a perm. The first time I permed my hair was at home. My sister did the honors. I waited almost an hour to get my hair straight, but when it was finally finished, my hair was still a little nappy. Whenever my sister would perm my hair, the perm would only stay in for about four days (as long as I didn't wash it).

I began to think my sister's perms were useless, so I pleaded with my mother to let me go to a salon. For a while she let me get a regular perm like everyone else—but this didn't last. My mother didn't want to pay $45 every six weeks for something that she objected to and that was damaging my hair.

By the time I was a freshman in high school, I had begun to think that I would never fit the image of the light-complexioned teen with soft, curly hair. Feeling frustrated about changing my looks, I began to question whether I was really the one who needed the change. I began to feel frustrated, too, at how caught up I had let myself get in these magazines and how caught up my friends still were.

After a while, instead of reading the articles, I found myself counting the number of white models compared to the number of non-whites. This was almost a daily ritual. My friends thought that I was crazy. A friend of mine who is half Indian and half black would say I was just jealous—she never understood why I was so upset. But, like me, most of my friends felt that they weren't perfect enough

Frustrated about my looks, I began to question whether I was really the one who needed the change.

and that their look wasn't acceptable. Lots of times they tried to correct these so-called problems by perming their hair, putting on a lot of makeup, and living in denial of their true identities— just like I had.

Now I'm 17 and I've hardly read any teen magazines in almost three years. I just couldn't bother with all the aggravation it took to try to be someone that I knew I wasn't and could never be. And I wasn't going to waste my time and money reading magazines that weren't interested in me.

Sometimes I do miss reading quizzes like "10 Love Lies," and "Is He the One for You?" There are times when I wish that I could forget about being left out and just lie back on my bed and read a funny story or check out the fashion do's and don'ts. But until I can open up a teen magazine and see a dark-skinned girl with her hair in dreads or just natural, with her 10 dark-skinned friends standing next to her, I'll have to get my laughs from the funnies.

Samantha was 17 when she wrote this story.
She later graduated from the University of Michigan.

James Faber

The Whitest Black Girl

By Nicole Hawkins

"What are you?"

When I was a little girl, kids used to ask me this question all the time. At first I would be surprised. Then I'd answer, "I'm black and Puerto Rican." I thought this would satisfy their inquiry, but I could see the rejection of my answer in their eyes. "No you're not," they'd say. "You're white."

I remember the first time this happened, on a cool autumn day in 1st grade. My classmates and I were doing our assigned work. All of a sudden one of them started shouting.

"White girl, white girl, Nicole's a white girl!" she yelled.

"No, I'm not. My daddy is black and my mommy is Puerto Rican," I said.

"No, you're not," she screamed. "You're white, look how light you are."

Then she started to laugh. I looked at my arm. I was white. She was right. I began to cry. I had my father, who is 6'4" and has a reddish-brown complexion, pick me up from school the next day. He made that girl feel oh so stupid, and helped me win my argument. Still, a couple of days later, the girl was at it again, calling me white girl. It didn't bother me as much as the first time, though. My skin was starting to grow thick.

As a biracial child, there's a certain tolerance level you have to build up to protect your feelings, because you're constantly being asked to choose one side

Half of me being recognized is just as bad as none of me being recognized. I'm black and Puerto Rican.

or the other. Growing up, whenever I had to fill out a form I'd be forced to choose between black (non-Hispanic), Hispanic (non-black), and Other. "Pick one only" was often written in bold letters. Sometimes I chose "Other," but usually I'd check black and Hispanic both. Later, I'd find that I'd been registered only as black, as though someone else had picked for me.

But it's not just strangers who want you to choose. It's your family, friends, and colleagues, too, whose little comments here and there choose for you. If I'm discussing something with my best friend, and we're having a disagreement, she'll say jokingly, "What would you know about that, white girl?"

Even my 15-year-old niece, who's Puerto Rican, defines me most of the time by calling me black girl. She doesn't call me Tia Nicole or Aunt Nicole, she calls me black girl. One day she said, "You know, you're the whitest black girl I know." Now when she said this, I wasn't mad at her, because she simply said out loud what other people think. The question in my mind was, "Why does she feel the need to label me?"

I suppose that ever since black people were forced to come to this country, in some way or other their biracial descendants have been forced to label themselves. Mulatto, mutt, confused, mixed, biracial, and multicultural are among the many names used to describe people of mixed race. History tells us how black people were brought here unwillingly, beaten, chained, and stripped of their culture. History tells us how these "mixed" children got here, too. In the beginning it was usually by force—the white master raped the black slave. Sometimes it was adultery, possibly love.

Sometimes the white masters made the biracial offspring their house slaves, and gave them the tiniest bit more freedom and respect due to their lighter complexion. This added to the resentment that field slaves carried for their lighter sisters and brothers. After the Civil War, black people with lighter complexions had some advantages, too.

Black sororities and fraternities segregated based on the different shades of black. Very light-skinned black people would sometimes try to "pass" as white, so they could receive economic, social, and educational advantages they would have otherwise been denied. Some black people even went so far as to bleach their skin.

Even now, I guess I do experience a different degree of discrimination than my darker counterparts. For example, at my job, I am able to listen in on and even be a part of race discussions with white people that they wouldn't have around someone darker than I am. And sometimes I think some white people feel more comfortable with me than with darker-skinned blacks. I don't think it's really conscious. It's just that a part of them relaxes because we share a common resemblance, our skin.

Perhaps that's why some black people may be offended by my color, and so they want me to declare who I really am. But I don't want to choose. It makes me angry when people call me white girl because I know that that's not true. Besides, if my black friends call me white girl, what they really mean is "bad."

It also makes me angry when people call me black girl, 'cause that's not true either. When my friends call me black girl, usually I feel loved, for a moment, because that means they've accepted me. But in the next moment, I feel invisible. Half of me being recognized is just as bad as none of me being recognized. I'm black *and* Puerto Rican.

I think we're so used to thinking in terms of black and white in this country that often people can't understand when there's something, or someone, in between. And because they can't understand me, they try to alienate me. Kind of like when you were a kid and you were bad at a subject and earned low grades. What came out of your mouth when you mother asked you why? "I hate that subject. I hate that teacher. She's mean." Because you couldn't understand the subject, you rejected it.

Part of me loved having two Thanksgiving dinners, and two cultures to call my own.

Maybe for people to feel secure with themselves and their heritage, they have to know who they're dealing with. Boundaries have to be set. Are you black or white? You can't be both. How do I socialize with you if I don't know how to cast you? But I think if we're going to define ourselves, we have to get past the black/white divide, and past the color of our skin.

Now that I'm older and I have a better understanding of my whole culture, I proudly state who I am. When people ask me the "what are you" question, I respond, "I'm blessed!" And I do feel blessed because I have a rich cultural background. A big part of my identity comes from my father, because we were always close. As a little girl, my father would tell me things about my ancestors that filled my heart with pride. Even though I was always closest to my father growing up, I was closer with my mother's side of the family.

My mother was the ninth of 15 kids. Needless to say, I have lots of cousins and they keep coming. My grandfather came to America from Puerto Rico to become a doctor, but changed his mind after he found God. Manuel T. Sanchez became a minister. Together he and my grandmother, Pilar, built their church, Iglesia Antioqua, with sweat, determination, faith, and love. Today the church still stands on Atlantic Avenue in Brooklyn.

On Thanksgiving, my mother's huge family would come together at my Grandma Pilar's house. Aside from the turkey, stuffing, and cranberry sauce, there'd be arroz con gandules (rice with beans) and benin (baked pork). Salsa and merengue would float through the air as the kids played hide-and-go-seek.

Later that night, my sister and I would visit my father's mother, who lived right across the hall from us—my grandma Hawkins. A second after we walked through the door, my cheeks would be torn from my face, my head would be rubbed, and I would grow dizzy from being tossed in the air. My grandma would ask me if I wanted food with funny names like chitlins, collard greens, and yams. Once all the food was on my plate, I would try my best to find somewhere to put it. After all, my stomach was already swollen from the afternoon.

But part of me loved having two Thanksgiving dinners, and two cultures to call my own. Hearing my grandma Hawkins' sweet southern voice, hugging her big, soft body, hearing my abuela call me "Nicolasa," is part of me. So is racing to the front door knowing that this tall brown man is my Daddy, and staring into my mother's beautiful green eyes. Knowing that my ancestors were kings and queens, black and beautiful, Spanish and strong, is part of who I am. It's a feeling that I have inside that tells me, "You are who you are, and that's uniquely you."

Nicole was 18 when she wrote this story.

John Morgan

Barack Is Black

By April Daley

You are not black. You are not white. You are not Asian. You are not whatever race you thought you were when you began reading this article. Why not? Because I just decided that you don't fit the stereotype. You're too "out of touch with your demographic." In fact, you're a lot like President Barack Obama.

Apparently, Obama isn't black. At least that's what columnist Stanley Crouch and others suggested when Obama was running for president. I disagree. I believe that Barack Obama is "black enough" and that no one has the right to question his race. I should know. I'm black, and people have been calling me things like "white girl" and "Oreo" my whole life.

The argument against Obama's "blackness" starts when he opens his mouth. Because he speaks elegantly, he's "talking white" in some people's eyes. I can relate. Back in 5th grade, I got called white whenever I answered a question correctly that no one else got right, or when I had all my homework ready to hand in. I didn't use much slang and that made it worse. Even now, when I speak to some black teens—acquaintances and neighbors—they say I talk like a white person.

People attack Obama's wardrobe as well. Because he dresses professionally, he's accused of "dressing white." He defies the stereotype that all black men wear clothes that are three sizes too big and can't form a sentence without the words "yo" and "nigga." I know what that's like, too.

Do you only qualify as black if you fit the stereotype: a thug who lives in poverty?

I get told I'm not black enough because I wear H&M and Aéropostale instead of Rocawear and Baby Phat and because I like more pop and rock artists than r&b and rap artists.

Another argument against Obama's blackness is that he's the child of a black immigrant and not a true member of black America, so he can't "identify." That idea implies that the experience of thousands of black immigrants in the U.S. is insignificant, like they don't also experience struggle and discrimination.

I was raised by Jamaican immigrants. Like Obama, the way that I live, dress, and speak is different from some black Americans. The culture my parents raised me in isn't exactly like the one that many black children here were raised in. But as much as the black kids called me "white" growing up, I am not white and I've had to deal with racism just like any black person in this country.

Like me, if Obama were to walk down the street of any city in any state in this country, as a regular citizen and not as the president, he would be classified as black. Not as a black immigrant, but simply black. Like me, he would face the same hardships as any other black person on those streets. To the people he walked past, he would be black enough.

The argument about Obama's race picks up speed when the critics examine Obama's upbringing. Obama was born to an African father and a white mother. His stepfather is Indonesian, and he grew up in Hawaii and Indonesia. Critics say that he can't sympathize with the average black family because he was never in one.

It's true that Obama grew up differently from most Americans—black or white. But that doesn't mean he doesn't care about the issues important to many black and/or low-income families. In fact, he's been proving they matter to him for his entire career. One of the first things Obama did after graduating from college was move to Chicago to help direct a non-profit program that helped provide job training for residents of poor, largely black neighborhoods.

The most troubling thing about the argument that Obama isn't black is what it implies about our country's definition of blackness. Does being black simply refer to the color of your skin, or do you also need to adopt a certain type of speech and certain views? Do you only qualify as black if you fit the stereotype of what some Americans consider black: a thug who lives in poverty? Why did my 10- and 11-year-old classmates, who called me white for being smart, associate educational success with white America?

In 5th grade, I cried or got fiercely defensive when someone questioned my race. Now I ignore it because the people questioning me are set in their opinions, so I see no point in arguing. I like the person I am and that person is 100% black. I can look in a mirror and verify that fact, and I don't think anyone else has the right to take that away from me. They can't take it away from Obama, either.

Sure, Obama attended Occidental College, Columbia University, and then Harvard Law School, while a lot of black people don't have the chance to go college at all. But why does being extremely educated lower his status as a black man? We should be celebrating his education—and everything else about his success in life—not using it as evidence that he's not part of the black community.

April wrote this when she was 17. She went on to study journalism at Northwestern University.

John Morgan

Barack Is Black...But Not African-American

By Donald Moore

Barack Obama is regarded as the first African-American president. But what exactly does "African-American" mean? And does Obama fit the definition? I don't think so.

This might be confusing to some. If you take the two words that make up the term "African-American" at face value, then you might assume he is. Yes, his father is a black Kenyan, and Obama was born in Hawaii, so it would seem that he fits the description. But the literal definition of a word and what people take it to mean can be worlds apart.

In no way am I saying that African-Americans shouldn't support Obama. But during the campaign, when *Time* magazine ran a story titled, "Can Obama Count on the Black Vote?" it implied that the black American vote is somehow more Obama's than any other Democratic candidate's by right, simply because he's African-American like them. To me, this is at best half-true.

The term African-American came into use as early as the '60s, during the civil rights movement. During his famous "The Ballot or the Bullet" speech in the 1964, Malcolm X referred to "Twenty-two million African-Americans—that's what we are—Africans who are in America." As I understand it, the term, which came into more widespread use in the '80s, refers to blacks whose ancestors were African slaves brought to the U.S.

In 1988, Jesse Jackson, then a U.S. presidential candidate, urged Americans to use the term to refer to black Americans. "It puts us in our proper historical context," he said during a news conference, according to a 2004 *New York Times* article. "Every ethnic group in this country has a reference to some land base, some historical cultural base. African-Americans have hit that level of cultural maturity."

While Jackson never made it clear whether he meant all blacks or not, the implication that African-Americans, by definition, didn't have an historic land base before leads me to believe that he meant the descendants of African slaves. They called themselves African-American because most blacks in America had no way of knowing which country in Africa their ancestors came from. Obama knows exactly where his ancestors come from. So if he wanted to, he could call himself Kenyan-European-American, since his dad was from Kenya and his mom was a white woman from Kansas.

> **Obama doesn't share the experiences that give most blacks in America a common identity.**

But vocabulary isn't the most important issue here. When I say that Obama isn't African-American, what I really mean is that he doesn't share the experiences that give most blacks in America (whose ancestors were slaves in this country) a common identity. African-American columnist Stanley Crouch wrote in a November 2006 *New York Daily News* column, "When black

Americans refer to Obama as 'one of us,' I do not know what they are talking about."

Obama does consider himself African-American. He was quoted by the *New York Times* as saying "Some of the patterns of struggle and degradation that blacks here in the United States experienced aren't that different from the colonial experience in the Caribbean or the African continent." He added, "For me the term African-American really does fit. I'm African, I trace half of my heritage to Africa directly, and I'm American."

But for many black Americans, ancestral lines from Africa are not what has shaped their identity. It's not just race either, since most African-Americans are mixtures of black, white, and Native American. To me, it's more about shared hardships and history.

As descendants of slaves, we know little about our African history, ancestors, or culture, so we have created our own culture and customs specific to America. The Harlem Renaissance, the Black Power movement, and musical forms like jazz and hip-hop all arose from the unique history of African-Americans.

While Obama was raised in the U.S., he was raised in a very different environment than most African-American kids. More than half of African-Americans live in metropolitan areas, with the majority living in overwhelmingly black neighborhoods, according to the 2000 U.S. Census. Obama's parents, both college-educated, divorced when he was 2, and he lived with his white mother, who later married an Indonesian man. Obama spent four years attending private school in Indonesia, and later lived with his maternal grandparents in Hawaii. Growing up in a white household in Hawaii is something that I'm guessing not many African-Americans can relate to.

Issues that disproportionately affect African-Americans compared to the rest of the country—government aid programs, police brutality, public housing—most likely did not affect him in his youth. As a result, many media critics have come to think that he doesn't "get it" as well as an African-American candidate would. For example, in an opinion piece for Salon.com, Debra J. Dickerson wrote, "Black, in our political and social reality, means those descended from West African slaves. Voluntary immigrants of African descent are just that, voluntary immigrants with markedly different outlooks on the role of race in their lives and politics."

As an African-American whose parents are from the South, I see some validity in that argument. Last year, my father told me about when my grandfather decided to move north to seek a better life for his family. The white factory owner he worked for tried to persuade him to stay. When he realized that my grandfather wasn't going to change his mind, he told him, "If you leave and move north, don't even think about coming back."

It being Alabama in the 1950s, my grandfather knew better than to take the man's threat lightly. He moved north with his family and didn't return until the '80s, out of fear for his life. My father and most of his brothers and sisters never went back to the South to see their relatives and friends. That's the kind of experience I bet Barack Obama has never had, and one I imagine he couldn't relate to. For millions of older African-Americans, including my parents, the memories of racist Jim Crow laws and segregation are all too vivid, and might still affect their view of race and politics.

Is Barack black like me? Of course. But he isn't African-American like I am.

But regardless of how you define African-American, Obama does have the same views as most African-Americans on most social and domestic issues. A Gallup poll taken in 2003 showed that, like Obama, 70% of blacks favored affirmative action, compared to 44% of whites. Also, most African-Americans are Protestants, with 33% attending church regularly, as Obama does.

So, despite the differences in upbringing, Obama does have a lot in common with African-Americans. Just because he doesn't share the same background as most black Americans doesn't mean he isn't looking out for them. But it does mean he shouldn't assume that black Americans can automatically relate to him because he's the same race. Is Barack black like me? Of course. But he isn't African-American like I am.

Donald was 18 when he wrote this story. He later completed high school and went on to college.

Odessa Straub

Don't Follow the Leader

By Anonymous

Looking out the windows of the #3 subway train, I spot a familiar sign: Rockaway Ave. The doors open and I enter my world, my home: Brownsville, Brooklyn, one of the poorest neighborhoods in New York City.

Slowly I walk down the stairs, then push my way through the turnstile. As I step outside, I'm greeted with the smell of weed, and the sound of "Newport, come get your Newport right here" echoing through the street. Eyes gaze as I walk by. I walk fast. I'm sick of seeing those same fools drug dealing to the vulnerable or hustling on the corner.

Look straight, look ahead, and surpass the negativity. Don't get sucked up in their dimension. Keep a positive mindset, don't be one of them. Don't notice a thing.

Even after so many years, my trip home still aggravates

me. It's disturbing to see the black community in this state. The thieves and drug dealers hurt each other and our neighborhood to become so-called successful. Their pride comes in knowing that they put a loaf of bread on the table. Tell me this, though: How do you feel knowing what you had to do to get it?

African-Americans have gone through so much to gain our so-called equal rights. So why are so many of us living in run down apartments, cooped up in projects, depending on welfare, stashed up in prison and stuck in segregated communities like Brownsville?

Very few drug dealers make more than minimum wage.

To find out, I talked with a sociologist at Columbia University, Sudhir Venkatesh, who spent years observing Chicago drug dealers' daily struggles to get rich or die trying. A gang member on his way to prison even gave Venkatesh detailed notes he kept about his hustling business, including how much the gang paid everyone from lookouts to leaders.

People deal drugs because they believe there's tremendous opportunity to go from rags to riches, Venkatesh said. But in fact, only very few drug dealers make more than minimum wage. The gang leader Venkatesh met paid himself about $100,000 a year—or $66 an hour. (Sounds like a lot, but that's about what some experienced, unionized teachers make, when you include benefits like health care.) But the gang leader paid the three guys beneath him about $7 an hour and the street level dealers an average of $3.30 an hour—less than minimum wage, which was about $4.25 at that time.

"If you look at 100 drug dealers, 99 will make less than minimum wage. One will make a lot of money. That's the reality on the streets," Venkatesh told me. "It's an illusion that people have that they're going to make a lot of money. That's only the leaders driving a fancy car."

Venkatesh said that he believes teens don't choose a life of crime so much as find it difficult to get a decent job. Many

African-Americans and Latinos grow up in poor neighborhoods like Brownsville where the schools usually do a poor job of preparing kids for decent jobs or college, he said. Most high-paying factory and union jobs have disappeared, so it's much harder to support a family without an education these days. And college has gotten expensive.

Racial discrimination and segregation also make it harder for minorities to start their own businesses, because many banks are unlikely to give loans to people who want to start businesses in poor neighborhoods, Venkatesh said.

Diane Hawkins-Bonaventure, deputy executive director of the nonprofit East New York Development Corporation, helps people who were on welfare get jobs. "It's always difficult for people to find jobs, but I work in the minority community, with people who've been on public assistance, and a lot—not all, but a lot—are lacking minimal education, like a GED, and have low or no marketable job skills, so it's really hard," she said.

Many of the drug dealers Venkatesh met seemed miserable standing out on the corner but couldn't see a way out. "Drug dealers are very, very scared. They don't like standing on a corner, they don't like carrying a gun. They don't know what's happening in their lives, but they're too scared to tell anybody. It's hard for them to ask for help," he said.

Poor teens get stuck on corners or in jail because we see the successful drug dealers flossing their platinum chains and spinning chromes on their Cadillacs, and we follow them. In other neighborhoods, kids see people become filthy rich by going to business school and putting on a suit.

One day I walked through Brooklyn Heights, a wealthy, mostly white neighborhood that's also in New York City. I wondered what kind of dreams the kids I know might have if they got off the train there. The neighborhood was almost picture perfect—the sidewalks weren't smothered with litter, the houses were old but not worn down, there wasn't any graffiti on the buildings.

I felt like I could breathe. I didn't have to worry about getting into an argument with any chickenheads. The streets weren't crowded, and when I spotted people they were minding their own damn business. I had no worries about my safety at all.

In that neighborhood, it's easy for kids to see the connection between getting an education and making money. In Brooklyn Heights, 58 percent of people over 25 have at least a college degree, and the average household income is $56,300, according to the 2000 Census.

Poor teens can succeed if they get help from after-school programs, social workers, and mentors.

Compare that to Brownsville, where only 8% have a college degree and the average household income is about $21,000. There aren't a lot of role models in my neighborhood to show kids like me the path to success.

The reality is that most children follow the examples of their parents and the people around them. That came home to me when I visited Norwalk, a small city in Connecticut. Riding the commuter train, I was shocked to look out the window and see enormous houses and green lawns. I usually see places like that on television, but here I was just an hour away from Manhattan. It all looked so beautiful.

When I talked to several groups of suburban teens, it struck me that all of them were expecting to go to college. For them, college wasn't an option, it was a must. They were probably so confident about college because their parents went, or their friends' parents went, and everyone around them expected them to go.

A lot of the kids in my school view college as a luxury. Everyone around us is doing so poorly that we tell ourselves, "I guess I can't break through these barriers," and we don't dare to.

When I asked Venkatesh and Hawkins-Bonaventure how they thought poor neighborhoods could change, they agreed that poor people of all ages need to come together and demand more from our government and business leaders, like a higher minimum wage and more job training.

"Advocate for change—change in schools, change in police patrols. Become more involved in what's going on in the community," Hawkins-Bonaventure said. "Go to your state representatives, city representatives, federal representatives and let them know what's needed."

They also agreed that poor teens can succeed if they get help from afterschool programs, social workers, and mentors who can show them a different path. Programs like the East New York Development Corporation already offer gang awareness and educational and recreational programs that encourage youth to stay out of trouble and in school. The large afterschool program offers help with homework and SATs, GED preparation for young adults, and a safe environment for youth after school.

Although I grew up in foster care in a hostile neighborhood, I've sought out other opportunities, like the debate team at my school and an after-school writing program. These experiences have shown me that I can look beyond the barriers I see between my dreams and me.

I know life can be really hard, and the future can seem like it's got nothing in it. It hasn't been easy trying to keep my head on in school so I can make it out. But I've used my disgust with my neighborhood and our society to become the total opposite. I wish that it could be easier for others to do the same.

The author was 18 when she wrote this story. She graduated from high school and went on to study social work in college, while holding several jobs.

Elizabeth Deegan

Big, Black, and Beautiful

By Anonymous

It took me a long time to convince myself that I am a beautiful girl. I grew up going to a private school where I was one of only a few black students. At that school, it seemed like only the thin, blond, and big-chested girls were considered appealing.

I am truly a brick house and have been called thick many times. No matter how fit I was, people regularly commented on my size because I wasn't thin and didn't look like a supermodel. Some students would talk about my round butt, thick hair and lips, and shapely figure. "Nobody wants your fat butt," one guy told me. I constantly worried about my physical appearance as a result. Whenever I'd get around friends I'd ask, "How does my hair look?" or, "Do I look fat in this outfit?" I was becoming almost annoying.

Because of the comments about my body, I often felt hurt, sad, and angry. Even if my friends and family told me how pretty, smart, or popular I was, the weight slurs would go straight to my head. I'd try to defend myself, but that would only make them bother me even more. They knew the slurs would hurt me, even if what they said was not true.

I felt so bad about myself that when attractive black guys looked at me, I'd turn my head and look the other way. I thought I knew what they wanted—white girls, Hispanic girls, or light-skinned black girls with long legs and straight hair. But at the same time, I'd get whistles and catcalls from black and Hispanic guys on the street who said complimentary things about my body. I'd wonder why they bothered. I was the big girl, the fat one.

I wanted to please the white guys and look and act the way they wanted me to.

It hurt the most when the boys would call me fat. Most of the guys in my school were white. The ones who weren't liked white girls, or at least the girls who looked like white girls. And since there weren't many black guys in my school, I wanted to please the white guys and look and act the way they wanted me to.

However, when I hung out with black friends outside of school I had to try to act cool, maybe even throw in some slang. But I sounded so stupid that I got picked on even more. I was always called the "white girl" whenever I was around my family or my black friends who didn't go to my school. "Do you think you have thin lips?" or "Why do you fling your hair like that?" they would ask. I'd try to ignore their comments, which were about everything from my legs to my hair. But it was hard.

Once, when a friend noticed I was shaving my legs, she looked at me disapprovingly and said, "Black girls don't shave their legs!" I asked her what she meant by that and she said, "Black guys think hairy legs are sexy." I don't think that's always true, or that it even matters. My friend also told me that "respect-able black women don't show off their stomachs either." Why couldn't she just ask me not to wear that shirt because she didn't like it, instead of making it into a race issue?

I felt as though one day couldn't pass without my friends and family mocking something I did that was totally natural for me. They made a race issue out of my looks, my voice, how I pronounced words, and everything I did. Their remarks always offended me. What did they mean, talking like a white girl? It was ridiculous! I was proud of the education I got at my school. I didn't know how to talk or act in any other way.

I know it doesn't have to be that way. Last summer I visited Spelman College, a historically black women's college in Atlanta, Georgia. The alumni there were extremely smart and had perfect diction. They were also proud of being black and were sure of their culture. They showed me that a black person can be and sound educated without losing her black identity. But in my old school, and with my friends and family, that didn't seem to be the case.

Finally, I got fed up and decided to transfer to a different school. I was tired of being examined and analyzed by everyone. Shortly after I arrived at my new high school, I began to have a whole new outlook on life. I noticed girls of all different sizes had boyfriends, and fine ones, too. "How did she get him? Look at her size," I would think. Walking the halls, guys commented on girls' butts—but not the way I was used to.

At the new school, no one commented on the way I talked, acted, or dressed.

"Look at how round it is, that's so fly," they'd say.

I was really shocked. These guys liked big butts and girls like me? Wow! I began to forget about my looks and could concentrate on my schoolwork. At the new school, no one commented on the way I talked, acted, or dressed. I was kind of expecting them to say something, but they didn't. I'm not sure if I was losing my "white girl" character, or if they just didn't care.

After a while, I began to compare myself to other black

females in my life. Many of my black girl friends love themselves, regardless of what size they are. Where did they get such positive attitudes? My white girl friends from the private school continuously complained about their size and thought they had to be thin to be accepted by men.

It would be great if more white girls had the same positive body image as many black girls. It also would be great if black girls could feel good about showing how educated they are, and would take a lesson from successful black women like the alumni I met at Spelman. Speaking and acting educated doesn't have anything to do with being white or black. I found out I don't have to look like a white girl or talk like a black girl. It may be best to be right in the middle.

The author was 17 when she wrote this story.

Dante Gutierrez

The N-Word

By Desiree Bailey

"Nigga, please."

My friend Jeff and I were having a slight disagreement at school last month when he decided to call me the N-word. Since we're both black, he somehow thought it was appropriate. But it's not to me. I hate to be referred to in that way by anyone, no matter what his race.

"Don't you ever call me a nigga," I said. And so our heated discussion began.

To Jeff, using the N-word within the black community is a way to turn the negative word "nigger" into a positive one. He told me that it's empowering to be able lessen the effect of a word created to demoralize blacks by changing its meaning. He claims that using the word allows it to roll off his back.

I've heard Jeff's argument a million times before from almost everyone who uses the word, in my life and on TV. I understand his point but I don't agree with it at all. There is no way that the word "nigga" can be empowering for me. I come from a strict Trinidadian household where pride in oneself and one's race is strongly encouraged. My parents always taught my brother and me to love and respect ourselves. They would have a heart attack if they heard us referring to people we care about as "niggas."

There is no way that the word "nigga" can be empowering for me.

That doesn't mean I haven't heard the word used in my house. Unfortunately, I have. But my relatives have only used it during rare moments of extreme frustration to describe a low, shameless character that betrayed them. In my house, the term is meant to degrade. But I don't approve of its use for that purpose, either.

I appreciated it when the New York City Council passed a resolution in 2007 to discourage the use of the N-word. (A resolution isn't a law; it's only intended to raise awareness.) The council recognized the word's painful past.

I was curious to learn more about the N-word, its origins and its source of power. I was also interested in the different viewpoints on its usage. So I started reading *The N Word: Who Can Say It, Who Shouldn't and Why,* a book by *Washington Post* Deputy Book Editor Jabari Asim. In his book, which was published in 2007, Asim chronicled the N-word's influence from its emergence in the U.S. to today's youth culture.

Asim wrote that the word "nigger" comes from "niger," the Latin word for "black," noting there is some dispute as to whether the word began as a neutral or derogatory term. One of the earliest written references of the word in the U.S. was in 1619 by colonist John Rolfe. It began as a description for black people. Since black people were scarcely thought about in a positive light, it was never used in a pleasant way.

The word became a way to intimidate and belittle blacks, and that continued into the 20th century, according to the book. In the 1930s there was a city limits sign in Hawthorne, California, that read, "Nigger, Don't Let the Sun Set on YOU in Hawthorne." That sounds like a death threat to me.

Asim suggested that the N-word is a metaphor for many low periods in black history. It represents white people's control over and contempt for blacks in the past. Blacks were once thought of as creatures and specimens. In the 1800s, there was even a false branch of science called "niggerology," in which unbelievable claims about blacks were accepted as facts. Blacks were thought of as the scum of society and in some cases, they still are. The N-word is a symbol for that long and horrible history of oppression. That's why I hate to see the word used as a term of affection or "brotherly love."

I think that calling your friends "niggas" makes a mockery of the past. How can other races take black people seriously when we use such degrading language to describe ourselves?

These days, kids hear people using the N-word in their community and start using it without stopping to think what the word really means. Black entertainers, many of whom probably heard the word growing up, use it in their work. Sadly, teens I know also hear their favorite artists and celebrities using the word so they think it's OK to use it.

But black people are still outraged when a white person calls them that name. Why? Because the word remains negative. So how is the "turning negative into positive" plan working there? I told Jeff that lifting ourselves out of the ghetto or any other bad predicament is what's empowering, not using a word that was created to keep us down.

I tried to explain to Jeff why I felt so strongly. "When I hear the word 'nigga' or 'nigger,' I see images of men like my father or my brother being hanged from a tree or kicked to death on the ground!" I told him.

While Jeff respected my point of view, he held his ground. I knew I couldn't change his mind in a matter of minutes, so we agreed to disagree. Trying to change his opinion would be as difficult and time-consuming as trying to de-program someone who's been brainwashed. I believe some blacks like Jeff have become desensitized to the word and to the struggles of our past. When we become desensitized, we run the risk of forgetting. And when we forget, we run the risk of repeating the torment through which blacks suffered.

> *Some blacks have become desensitized to the word and to the struggles of our past.*

While I don't think we should use the word in conversation, it should not be erased from the English language. The word should remain as a reminder of all the suffering blacks endured in the past. Instead of using the language of racists, blacks should use the memory of that word and everything surrounding it as fuel and motivation to get ahead.

They should hear the word and remember the dreams of blacks in the past like Toussaint L'Overture, Harriet Tubman, and many others who weren't honored in all of our history books. They should remember how many blacks risked their lives in slave revolts, the Underground Railroad, and the civil rights movement of the 1960s to give us a better future.

The N-word should remind African-Americans to resist racism and prejudice. And young blacks should pay respect to the past by dropping the word from their everyday speech. "Nigga" is not a word to be thrown around lightly.

Desiree wrote this story when she was 18. She graduated high school and enrolled at Georgetown University.

Jovanny Canizares

Singled Out

By Angelina Darrisaw

In 7th grade I was the only black girl in my class, and it was strange. I knew my new school was going to be predominantly white, but I didn't realize I'd be the only black person in my grade for two years.

I'm from a black neighborhood, and even though I knew I had a few white relatives, I had little interaction with white people until 7th grade. Before then, I went to an all-black public school where I got joked on for being light-skinned and having long, wavy hair. My old classmates had called me white girl, but at my new school it was instantly clear that I was a black girl—surrounded by actual white girls.

I ended up at my school though a program that places gifted children, mostly of color, into private schools. My mom put me through the 14-month program because she saw it as an educational opportunity. I applied and got accepted to the school I attend now. My mom chose it because it was small, with only about 400 students from nursery to 12th grade. We also felt, after our visits, that it was less snooty than others and that its Catholic background gave it a warm feel.

I was shy at first. But my classmates were so friendly it was easy for me to open up. They asked about my old school, my family, the shows I liked, and my hobbies. Still, sometimes I felt they were asking those questions out of duty, not out of interest.

Even though my white classmates were generally friendly, they kept me aware that I was the only black girl. Sometimes it was like I represented the entire black race. Whenever anyone mentioned someone black or something about being black, my class would look at me. Classmates asked me, "What do black people like to be called, African-American or black?" I told them, "I can only speak for myself."

Classmates asked me, "What do black people like to be called, African-American or black?" I told them, "I can only speak for myself."

I was the only black girl in my class, but there were a few other black students in the school. The administration made two of them, a senior and a junior, talk to me weekly, claiming it was because I was new. But none of the other new girls met with two older students. It was just me. Meeting with those girls helped because we shared experiences and they dropped knowledge, but it only added to my feeling of being separate and different.

My classmates seemed to assume that I and other black girls lived in some TV-type ghetto where everyone was a gang member and I had to dodge bullets to get home. My neighborhood is actually quiet most of the time and people keep to themselves. Some comments were so ignorant I had to laugh about it later, though I still found them offensive. I was amazed my school-mates could be that sheltered. A lot of people also assumed that all the minority kids were on financial aid, which wasn't the case.

It was the more general statements about poor people and blacks that killed me, though, like, "Most people on welfare are black," which isn't true. It was clear we had different realities. My life was something they could only hear about and wouldn't dream of living. And it was weird because I thought I was better off than a lot of kids in my city. But because I didn't have a maid and designer clothes, I was poor by their standards.

Our different backgrounds led us to different political opinions, too. Most of the girls were pro-Republican and pro-rich. At my old school, it was the opposite. So I was shocked to discover that people could favor programs and government officials who I thought cared little for most of the city's residents.

I got into heated debates with some of my classmates about the problems with our capitalist system, or why affirmative action could be justified, or how slavery was no fault of Africans. It was frustrating, not just to come up against opinions I thought were wrong, but to be the only one with my opinions. I had to constantly defend my perspective.

Our different upbringings made it hard to relate on some issues, but girls are girls. We liked boys, food, music, and going out, so sometimes we could connect on that level. But then differences still remained. I preferred black boys, they preferred white boys. They'd meet guys at the joint school dances with private all-girl and all-boy schools. I could count on one hand how many black guys went there, so I'd meet guys through my old school, my neighborhood, or my church. We also had different ideas of what was fun. A lot of them smoked, drank, or shopped for fun. My friends and I danced and went to movies for our fun.

Maybe it's because of these differences that my classmates didn't invite me to their parties and dances. One of them told me at the end of 7th grade, when I asked her why I didn't get invited to her party, that they didn't invite me because they felt I would be uninterested. I wasn't sure what she meant by that, but I think if I'd been invited, I'd have gone without hesitation. I wanted to have friends in a new school like everybody else. It hurt to be left out.

Not having any good friends at school and always feeling alone made me miserable. I felt like I was in kindergarten all over again, being called white girl and excluded from playing double-dutch. But now I was excluded because I was black. By the end of the year I'd had enough. I really wanted to change schools and sometimes came home in tears because I hated my school so much.

"Mommy, I can't take it anymore," I screamed at home one day. "Come on! Let me go to another school, puhleeeeeeze!"

Mom wasn't hearing that. "Sweetie, I know it can get tough, but what do you think the real world is going to be like? No matter where you go, there's going to be problems and I don't want you changing schools. End of story."

I thought she was just making excuses, and that she didn't want me to change schools because the admission process had been so hard. But down deep, I knew she was right. I could stick it out.

The following year, I was nominated to be a class representative, much to my surprise. I guess my classmates liked the way I spoke my mind and had an opinion on everything, because I was elected. That made me feel less alienated and more liked. But I still wasn't cool enough for anyone in my class to invite me to hang. I had to take the initiative and invite them downtown or to a movie. Sometimes they joined me, but I felt like a friendship shouldn't be so one-sided.

So I was happy to connect with the few other black students in the grades above me. We made an effort to call each other and really be friends—in school and out. We came from a variety of backgrounds and classes, but our cultural similarities—and our experience of feeling excluded—brought us together.

At lunch, we often sat at the same table in the teahouse (my school's version of a cafeteria) every day. It's not like we had a sign that said "No Whites Allowed!" But some people at school thought we were excluding others. The administration told us to break it up. It became a whole big drama questioning why the black kids were always together, but we saw it as white people always sitting together. We, who connected after being excluded, were told that we were excluding people. We were just friends who liked being with each other and were rarely invited to sit with white schoolmates, so why couldn't we be together?

> *It's not like we had a sign that said "No Whites Allowed!" But some people thought we were excluding others.*

The drama continued into my freshman year, with assemblies and student-teacher groups organized to discuss how people felt about the issue. Many students, black and white, didn't think it was such a big deal. We thought the teachers were overdoing it. We made more of an effort to mix with the white students, but most of the time, we still sat together.

If I could do prep school over again, I probably wouldn't. But as I'm getting older, I see that I have to make the best of it, or at least try to. Knowing hundreds of other kids are going through the same thing makes it easier because there's always someone to talk to. And while going to an elite private school is often a strain socially, academically I'm happy. I've taken fantastic classes in literature and modern world history and participated in a model congress.

This September marks my fourth year there. And soon, I'm going to be the junior or senior who's asked to talk to the shy, new black 7th grader. I guess I'll just say, "Hey, I'm always here to talk.

It gets hard sometimes, but being here, you get opportunities that will be really important in the long run. Remember, you're in school to learn. And you gotta make yourself happy."

Angelina was 15 when she wrote this story. After completing high school, she graduated from Davidson College and enrolled in business school at Wake Forest.

Elizabeth Deegan

The Flag's Not for Me

By Anonymous

I used to be proud to be an American. When I was around 4 or 5, my mother bought me a T-shirt of the flag. The shoulder and breast pocket had a vibrant blue background with white stars, and red and white stripes streamed down the rest of the shirt. I loved to wear it, and felt so proud when I did. That flag shirt made me feel a little something extra, like I was part of something special.

But my pride for that star-spangled banner has become bruised as I've gotten older. I no longer wear the flag, or wave the flag, because it doesn't feel like it symbolizes something real. To me, the flag is supposed to represent fairness and equality for everyone, regardless of your race, religion, or social standing.

When people say the flag stands for "liberty and justice for all" during our pledge of allegiance, I question the use of the word "all," because it often doesn't include women or blacks or other minorities. So many people are treated unfairly in this country by the system or by other individuals. I wouldn't feel right walking around with my head held high for the U.S. when I've seen TV reports of Arabic people in the U.S. being persecuted, even though they're supposed to be in a country where everyone's treated fairly.

When terrorist Timothy McVeigh, a white man, bombed a federal building in Oklahoma City in 1995, there were no reported incidents of white people being victimized just because they were the same race as McVeigh. But when the World Trade Center attack occurred, many Muslims, Arabs, and people who looked like they might be were persecuted because the terrorists were Muslim. That's just unfair. It appears to me that if you're not part of the majority, then you're open to discrimination and social brutality.

Our legal system allows officers to gun down innocent men and receive no punishment.

I look at recent history and see individual examples of bias and prejudice. Matthew Shepard, a young homosexual male in Wyoming, was beaten to death in 1998 for being gay. Even though the men who committed the atrocity were imprisoned, it still doesn't change the fact that Shepard is dead because his attackers objected to his right to express himself.

Then there are the wrongs that have historically been committed upon blacks in this country. Blacks have had to deal with centuries of civil injustice spawned by slavery. And after years of segregation, sit-ins, marches, boycotts, and being hosed down in the streets, we're still struggling.

I'm disgusted by the instances of racial profiling and police brutality that have been documented. When I saw the video of the Rodney King beating, I was 6 and puzzled by what happened to him. I first thought that I was watching a clip from the '60s during the civil rights movement, when African-Americans in the South were beaten by police. But in actuality, I was watching a mob of Los Angeles police officers beating an unarmed black man on the street. Later, the four cops accused of beating King were acquitted of assault charges by a state jury, while only two of the four were found guilty by a federal jury for civil rights violations.

Eight years later, in 1999, Amadou Diallo was murdered by the New York City police. That really opened my eyes to the real world of America, a world where a man was shot 41 times in the entrance of his home because police thought he had a gun. When I heard what happened, I was shocked, despite previous instances of brutality I knew about. My mind was reduced to a ball of confusion, particularly after the outcome of the trial, in which all the officers got off scot-free because they said they believed their lives were on the line.

The same thing happened again in New York in 2006 when Sean Bell, an African-American man who was unarmed, was shot to death by police officers the night before his wedding. The officers went to trial but were found not guilty. Our legal system allows officers to gun down innocent men and receive no punishment.

Why should I stand for the American flag if it does not stand for me?

I can't help but think that we as black men don't have the same rights as others. I'm saddened because sometimes it seems like you can't be black and American at the same time, sort of like Superman and Clark Kent; though they're the same person, they're viewed and treated as different entities by others.

So why should I stand for the American flag if it does not stand for me or my ideas of fairness for all? To wave the flag, I feel like I should be proud of all that it embodies and represents. While I know some say that minorities in this country are in a better place socially and economically than ever before, I can't wave the flag because we're still not receiving our fair share.

The American flag has been used as a mask to hide the true face of America, a face covered with blemishes of discrimination by the government and private citizens. We cannot fold over these pages of history where people are beaten or shot by individuals who're supposed to protect them. We should remedy these problems before we wave our flags and declare that we're in the land of the free.

The America I wish to live in is one where freedom and justice are truly for all. That's the America I want. That's the America I deserve!

The author was in high school when he wrote this story.

Lee Samuel

Where My Girls At?

By Danielle Chambers

Walking down the street I see a black boy who doesn't look older than 11. The boy has on sagging jeans and a large black hoodie and a new-looking pair of Tims. He's walking with white wires hanging from his ears.

I'm with a young girl from my neighborhood. She's 8 and telling me about how she scored 100 on her spelling test. I tell her how proud I am of her and how bright and beautiful she is.

She points out the boy and tells me how he's in the 6th grade and about how all the girls have a crush on him. The boy approaches, reciting the rhymes to the song he's listening to on his iPod, "These are my b-tches...my alpha b-tches...I get b-tches." I look down at her and ask her if she likes him. She looks at me like I'm crazy and says, "Ew, boys are disgusting!"

After that I go home and look up the song, and I'm angry when I find out it's by Lil Wayne, one of the most popular rappers today. I'm not so much angry that he wrote it as upset at who's listening to it. The audience of some of the most famous and "respected" rappers are boys like that 6th grader, and sometimes they're even younger.

What happens when that young girl decides she likes boys, I wonder. Are the boys going to cheat on her, abuse her, and call her a b-tch? What happens when Lil Wayne's daughter starts to like boys? Is this how he wants boys to treat his little girl?

Everywhere you look is another video with black women shaking their assets and another rapper talking about women like they're not even human.

Lil Wayne is far from alone in the way his music disrespects women. These kinds of messages are so common in hip-hop. Everywhere you look is another video with black women shaking their assets and another rapper talking about women like they're not even human. It not only hurts the self-esteem of the young girls and women, but conditions young black men to believe that women of color do not deserve respect. And that hurts our entire community. As Chris Rock says, "I love hip-hop, but I'm tired of defending it."

Rappers create and perpetuate many negative stereotypes of black women. They show black women as money-grubbing whores and uneducated. These stereotypes affect black women in every part of society.

Disrespecting black women has become so routine that a few years ago, a middle-aged white talk radio DJ named Don Imus felt he had the right to call black female basketball players at Rutgers University "nappy-headed hos." (Imus was fired from his job, but less than a year later he was back on the air.) Sadly, what Imus said is the same thing that people in hip-hop are saying about black women. I don't see anyone firing them from their jobs.

Hip-hop wasn't always this way. Women used to inspire and show the world a different side of what the hip-hop scene is all about. Female rappers spoke up and defended real women by flipping the script and taking sexuality into their own hands. Artists like Queen Latifah, Salt-N-Pepa, TLC, MC Lyte, and Lauryn Hill provided voices of female empowerment.

But many of those MCs are not around today. In fact, I can't think of any positive female MCs in mainstream hip-hop right now holding the ladies down. So where are all my girls at? What happened to the strong girl from around the way? Most of the women MCs have vanished. And in a world dominated by men, women are not treated with respect.

For example, "Superhead" became one of the most popular women in hip-hop, but not because of her skills on the mic. She wrote the notorious *Confessions of a Video Vixen* about all the rappers she slept with and how they mistreated her. *Confessions* was number one on the bestseller list. She's one of the most famous women in hip-hop because she played into the stereotype.

Mainstream female rappers like Lil' Kim and Foxy Brown are nice on the mic, but when was the last time anybody heard about a Foxy Brown album instead of a Foxy Brown court date? Lil' Kim, anyone? I think not. She used to be like hip-hop's Madonna, letting the world know that women were in control of their own sexuality rather than sexual objects that exist just to be handled by men. But her music just hasn't matured as she's gotten older. Retaliating against men by referring to them as objects isn't a solution. Lil' Kim's just a female version of the same old misogynistic messages perpetuated by male rappers.

For anyone who thinks that this is no big deal, I would argue that it's actually destroying the entire industry. There is a lack of individuality. All the rappers' beats sound the same and they're all rapping about the same things: money and b-tches. There's no innovation, just a pressure to make money. This is supposed to be our art form; it's part of our culture, embedded in the way we dress, talk, and even think. Generation hip-hop shouldn't be sacrificing women just for the sake of making a buck.

But I still hold out hope. Some rappers, like Andre 3000, Lupe Fiasco, Common, and T.I. write music that is cool and sounds good and has positive messages. They come from very distinct places and have swag all their own. They have fresh sounds that are completely different from the rest of the rappers in the game. Unfortunately, most of the other MCs with fame and clout, both male and female, are just making it hard for sistas out here.

And there are still strong women in hip-hop who can inspire today's youth. We need them to speak up about the beautiful black women in the real world who struggle every day to overcome these damaging stereotypes. There are many powerful black women who uplift our generation and use their gifts to help advance people of color. We live in an age of graceful, smart, and beautiful women like Michelle Obama, Maya Angelou, Condoleezza Rice, and Oprah Winfrey. But too often, the things they stand for and accomplish are ignored by society. My question is why, after years of struggle and accomplishments, women of color are still reduced to b-tches.

Get real. If you're a black woman, they mean you.

Many women say they listen to the lyrics but don't associate themselves with the negative, degrading things that the rappers say. Come on, get real. If you're a black woman, they mean you. Young black women should not subject themselves to what destroys them. Be choosy about the music you listen to, and don't support so-called artists who are putting out the same tired old messages.

The value of the black community is lowered by artists who

are in a position to advocate for change but do not. If we start choosing not to support them, maybe we'll be the ones to make a change for the better.

Danielle was 18 when she wrote this story.

John Morgan

My First White Friend

By Anita Ames

Meghan was the only white girl in my grade in junior high. She was a tall girl with dirty blond hair and she seemed nice. Although we'd been in school together since kindergarten, friendship with her had never crossed my mind. She was white, so what could we possibly have in common?

But in 6th grade Meghan was in my math class. She was really good at math, so one day I asked her for some help on a math problem. From then on, I found myself always asking her for help, playing basketball in gym with her, and talking with her about music. We discovered that we shared a love for Avril Lavigne, Eminem, and Mariah Carey. One day, our social studies teacher assigned a project and told us we could work in groups or alone. I decided to work with Meghan, not only because she was smart, but also because I wanted to get to her house to try the food.

I was curious about white people: How they lived, what they did, and most of all, what their food tasted like. My mom had told me that white people didn't use any seasoning and that their food was plain, but I wanted to try it for myself.

"Meghan honey, supper is ready," Meghan's mother called from downstairs the first evening I went to her house.

"Supper?" I thought. I'd only heard that word on TV. When we got downstairs, the table was set with a plate at every seat, along with a fork, knife, and napkin. My family never had dinner together, let alone set the table. Meghan's dad, brothers, and sister came downstairs. Her dad said grace, something else my family never did, and then her mom served us. Steak, squash, rice, and a baked potato.

It smelled really good, but when I cut my steak it was bleeding, and Meghan's mom served milk as a drink. I thought I was going to be sick. I hated milk with no cereal, and at home the steak never bled. "Ms. Susan, my steak isn't done," I said.

"Oh, it's medium rare. Do you want some steak sauce to make it better?" she said.

"Sure," I said, and I discovered that the steak was really good—even without the sauce. But at the end of dinner, I still hadn't finished that milk. Ms. Susan had to put chocolate in it to get me to drink it.

She was white, so what could we possibly have in common?

I never drank milk with dinner again, but after that, I remembered to always ask for medium rare burgers at restaurants. Some of Meghan's family's customs were different than what I was used to. But based on that dinner, I decided that white people's food was a new and good indulgence. And they did use seasoning.

Back at school, my black friends and I accepted Meghan as one of us. It was fun to interact and learn from someone of a different race. We taught her how to play double dutch at recess, and she joined our dance group and learned the hip-hop and reggae dances that we performed in talent shows. She danced well and even added in some steps for us to learn, which were more of a pop style but blended in well with the rest of the dance routines.

Meghan and I had differences, but most of them had nothing to do with race. I couldn't sleep with any light on, while Meghan had to sleep with the TV on. She couldn't brush her teeth before breakfast, and I had to brush my teeth as soon as I woke up. We didn't pay much attention to racial differences. But when we did notice any, we treated

I was curious about white people: How they lived, what they did, and what their food tasted like.

them with curiosity, like when I asked Meghan how she took care of her hair since it was a different texture from mine.

Meghan and I are still friends to this day, although since we go to different high schools we don't speak that often anymore. I've made other white friends since then and I know that Meghan doesn't represent all white people. But she was key to opening my eyes to other cultures and to trying new things. She taught me that white and black people may be different when it comes to culture and customs, but as individuals we can have a lot in common.

Anita was 16 when she wrote this story.
She later completed high school and went to college.

YC Art Dept.

Black Girl, White Campus

By Samantha Brown

For my entire childhood, most of my friends were either black or Hispanic. When I did have white and Asian friends, during my senior year in high school, I thought it was cool. I felt more conscious of race when I was talking to them, but I still felt free to say how I felt, and I was not afraid to act ghetto.

When I arrived at the University of Michigan, where most people are white, I was intrigued. I was conscious of my race, but I also felt comfortable. During the first week of the school year, the sororities and fraternities were having parties all around campus. One night I went with three girls from my dorm.

At first I was hesitant to go because I remembered all the warnings I had heard about people getting drunk and raped, becoming alcoholics and drug addicts, or just flunking out of school. My sister in particular had always warned me to be careful, but after thinking for a while, I said, "The hell with my sister," and went anyway.

At the sorority parties, I began to notice that there were hardly any minorities. People were drinking and laughing, and I saw the two white friends I had come with joining in. No one danced. They just drank beer and smoked weed. All the girls looked the same—dressed up in tight black dresses and hooker boots. I felt nervous. And I could tell that my friend Rae, who's also black, was nervous, too, because she kept holding on to my windbreaker. After the party, I was determined to find more black people.

I had been against affirmative action before I came to college. But once I came here and saw how white the campus was, I changed my mind. It made me angry that many of my white friends did not agree with affirmative action. I thought they were not in touch with the real world.

For instance, one of my friends said that there was equality in education between blacks and whites, and that it was all about working hard and getting the grades. I told her that she had never gone without textbooks because of government cutbacks, and

After the party, I was determined to find more black people.

never had to sit in a classroom with 40 students because there were hardly any teachers.

It was also frustrating to me that there were not that many cute black guys whom I could just chill with, and that I didn't hear any hip-hop music in the dorms. After a while, I made more black friends. I still have some white friends, and I'm especially close with my roommate, who's great. She listens to all of my complaints and is very understanding. She has even got me to listen—and like—some country music. But for the most part, I am better able to identify with my black friends, and, because there are so few of us, I think we need to stick together.

*Samantha was a freshman in college
when she wrote this story.*

Odessa Straub

Coloring Outside the Lines

By Desiree Bailey

I didn't think much about race until 7th grade, when I joined the gifted class at my school. For the first time, I was the only black person in my class, and I suddenly felt a lot of pressure. I thought that if I didn't do well, my classmates would think it was because I was black. Race suddenly mattered to me, and I felt completely out of place.

It was the first time I'd realized I was a minority. All my life I'd been around a diverse mix of people. On the island of Trinidad, where I was born, the population is mostly of African and Indian descent with a sprinkling of Chinese, Hispanics mainly from Venezuela, Native people (Caribs, Amerindians and Arawaks), and whites. It seemed to me that almost everyone there lived side by side.

In Rosedale, Queens—the New York City neighborhood that

I immigrated to when I was 8—almost everyone was black. My elementary school was mostly black, but there were also Indians from the Caribbean. Since my neighbors and classmates in New York were similar to the people I lived around in Trinidad, I still didn't think about race.

At home, race had never been a big issue for my mother. She'd acknowledge racial prejudice but she never dwelled on it. My father, on the other hand, came to America in the 1970s, when black people were struggling for equality and respect. He read a lot about the plight of blacks around the world, and kept us in endless conversations about it. In our kitchen, we even had a beautiful poster depicting all the great kings and queens of Africa's past. But the discussions were all theoretical to me. My real-life encounters with racism were rare.

When I first started 6th grade at a middle school in Bayside, Queens, my class had a mix of black, white, Asian, and Hispanic kids. There were only a few black kids, unlike my elementary school, which was probably 99.9% black. But I still felt at ease because there was such a diverse mix. So when I started 7th grade, being the only black kid in my class caught me by surprise. I couldn't blend in anymore. I was easily recognized as "the black kid," and I was afraid of the attention that I might get.

It was up to me to show my classmates that not all black people were loud and obnoxious.

I felt like I wasn't just representing myself, but all black people. For many of my classmates, I imagined I was the first black person they'd ever had a chance to get to know. I worried for the first time that many people didn't see blacks as individuals, but as a stereotype, a group of people who all acted the same: loud, uneducated, and obnoxious.

I assumed that my classmates had those prejudices, and I couldn't make a fool of myself in front of them. I imagined that one little mistake wouldn't just be mine; it would be the mistake of my race. The pressure I placed on myself made me hesitant to speak. What if I said the wrong thing? What if words flew tangled and contorted out of my nervous mouth? I became quiet. I became even quieter when the topic of black people came up. When we talked about slavery in social studies class, I wanted to disappear. Although I didn't spot any outward signs of racism, I still felt singled out.

My classmates were so cautious around me. When they described black people, they'd pause to search for the best word to use without being offensive. If they described someone white or Asian, I'd never hear that hesitation. Maybe it's because blacks have always had a sensitive position in America. Their self-censorship made me even more uncomfortable and aware of my differences.

Perhaps my insecurities about my people and myself were fueled by negative images of blacks in the media. In the movies I saw, young black men were almost always criminals, blazing a path of destruction wherever they went. In popular music videos, I saw women of all shades of brown exploited by their own black men. I felt like my race was a big show, a huge entertainment session intended to amuse, excite, and instill fear in others.

In my neighborhood, some people reinforced these ideas. It began to bug me that many of the black teenagers I saw on the bus were rude and obnoxious. They'd jump on the bus seats, shout at the top of their lungs and pick fights with each other, bothering innocent people who were minding their own business. Some women would walk around with barely any clothes on while men hooted at them. Many black people I saw seemed to be on edge and angry, or just looking for fun laced with trouble.

I wasn't like that. Instead of wreaking havoc on the bus, I'd quietly read my book. I wasn't rude or a troublemaker, and I didn't want my people to be seen that way. It's true there were many other black kids like me. Instead of hanging around the block, they read books like I did. And they were smart kids with bright futures. But I didn't meet those kids until high school. In 7th grade, I just wanted to fit in with the white and Asian kids in my class.

I decided that it was up to me to show my classmates that not all black people were loud and obnoxious. I'd teach them that black people could be successful and not like the negative characters that they saw on TV. I'd show them that we could enjoy different types of music and be as open-minded and cultured as anyone else.

In my quest to separate myself from the black stereotypes I thought my classmates expected to see in me, I began to reject things I identified as black. I didn't dare pick up a book by Maya Angelou. I avoided listening to hip-hop and r&b. The sounds from my headphones were from bands like Linkin Park, Staind, and System of a Down. If a band played rock, I listened to it. At first, I didn't even enjoy the heavier rock. But I wanted to like it, so I listened to it again and again until it became my love. I thought it would help me be more like my classmates. The confusion and swirls of the drums and guitars eventually came to reflect how I felt.

But no matter how hard I blasted my rock music, it didn't help me to fit in. My physical differences were clearly pointed out by my classmates. One day, a boy with pale skin and brownish-blond hair asked me about my hair. "Why is it like that?" he said. He looked at my neatly braided cornrows with a look more of disgust than curiosity. "It's so stiff and it looks like a bunch of train tracks are stuck to your head." I was extremely hurt by his comments. No one had ever been so rude about my race to my face. How could anyone be so obnoxious and unkind?

When I went to the house of another classmate, I felt even more stigmatized. Her mom was Puerto Rican and her dad was Chinese, and I didn't expect ignorant attitudes from a family with such diversity. But I heard her younger brothers whispering to each other about me. "Why is she so black?" one said. Another said, "Maybe if she scrubs her skin really hard, it'll come off." They walked into another room laughing while I stood there feeling insulted and uncomfortable. My friend acted as if nothing happened. So did I. I didn't want to make a scene.

Situations like that made me feel even more separated from my peers. I sank deeper and deeper into my rock music. But instead of helping me fit in with the white kids, my music separated me from the few black people I knew in other classes. One day, I was on the bus going home with two friends, one black and the other Hispanic. One asked what I was listening to, so I gave him my headphones. When he heard the ear-splitting drums of System of a Down and the monstrous growl of the lead singer, he looked at me like I was a joke.

I began to think that I was a racist—a racist against my own people.

"What the hell is that?" he asked. "Why are you listening to rock? That's white people music." I felt my face grow hot but I didn't know how to respond, so I just laughed his comments off.

All these conflicts upset me. I felt too black for the kids in my class and too white for my friends in other classes. I'd talk and laugh with people, but inside, I just wanted to get away from everyone. Every chance I got, I isolated myself and delved deeper into my books, my writing, and my music. They were my favorite places to escape.

It was hard to for me to realize who I was becoming until I became friends with Jessica in the 8th grade. She was obsessed with insulting her own dark brown skin. She was devastated because she thought she was hideous and wouldn't be loved by anyone. "I hate myself," she'd say. "I'm so black and ugly."

I didn't pay attention to her at first because I thought she was just fishing for compliments. But it didn't take me long to realize that she meant what she said. She'd look at my friend, Ashley, who was black but light-skinned, and say, "Why can't I be your color?"

Ashley and I worried about her. We told Jessica that skin color and beauty weren't connected, but it was hard to convince her when the media ambushed us with those ideas every day. We couldn't convince her she was wrong about herself, and she eventually withdrew from us.

Seeing how Jessica's negative thoughts destroyed her self-esteem, I began to wonder if I was doing the same thing to myself. When I reexamined my beliefs, I was shocked to realize that all the stereotypes I thought others believed about black people were things I believed. When I saw black people lazing on street corners, or behaving inappropriately in music videos, I shook my head with disgust. I thought back to all the past struggles and achievements of black people and wondered if my generation would flush it all down the drain.

Instead of looking into situations more deeply, I simply pointed my finger and criticized my people. I realized I was stereotyping my own people as rude and ignorant when I was the one who was rude and ignorant. I had poisoned myself against my race just to fit in with my classmates. I began to think that I was a racist—a racist against my own people.

I decided I couldn't let my fears decide my behavior or tastes anymore. I began to work hard to see people as individuals with interesting lives, instead of simplistic stereotypes.

It's taken several years to change my thinking. At times I still feel extremely different from other people, but now I see that as a good thing. My differences showed me the way to writing, playing the flute and guitar, and my interest in anthropology. I still have to deal with ignorance about black people from my white and Asian classmates, and ignorance from black people about my interests. Despite this, I'm committed to being myself instead of trying to represent an entire race. And I'm not going to judge my own race, or any other race, based on stereotypes.

Now I'm in 11th grade and I'm on great terms with myself as a black teenager. It doesn't bother me anymore if I'm seen as "too white" by some and "too black" by others. I know it's impossible to expect everyone to see the world exactly as I do.

My music collection covers Alicia Keys and Kanye West as well as Coldplay and Jimi Hendrix. Books by Maya Angelou, J.K. Rowling, and Pablo Neruda spill off my shelves. My music, my literature, and my perspective don't belong to a particular race. They don't have a specific color. They're just what I love.

Desiree wrote this story when she was 18. She graduated high school and enrolled at Georgetown University.

Kelvin Mclennon

Black Pride, and a New Ride

By Norman Brant

A few months ago, I was standing on line to get a movie ticket when, out of nowhere, this big silver object appeared in front of the theater like a UFO. It drove up slowly and without a sound. I couldn't help but stare at this beautiful mechanical creature resting so peacefully before me, and wonder what species it was. It was a Mercedes. I knew right then and there that no matter how long it took, I was going to ride in a new Mercedes. And I would make sure everyone knew about it, too.

If there's one thing I know about myself, it's that I have expensive taste. In my family, nice clothes and nice cars are important. Everyone's always showing off. Some people in my family work really hard to make good money and live a comfortable life. I think there's nothing wrong with wanting the best and working for it.

Unfortunately, other people in my family have gone about getting what they want in the wrong way. When I'd visit their homes, I'd think they were millionaires. Leather furniture, carpets in every room, the works. Of course, I liked everything about it, except how they got it—selling drugs. It's sad because most of them are now in jail, and all the riches they had are gone forever.

Unlike them, I am going to succeed in life the way the ministers, accountants, nurses, and executives in my family did—by working hard and getting an education. I want to have material things to prove I'm successful, so people who think a black man can't make it in America will see that they're wrong. I want to be able to feel proud of the things I own. But because I am a black male, I'm sure I'll experience unnecessary obstacles and insults to get what I want.

I'm not even 18, and I have already had to experience prejudice too many times. Often I have felt so disrespected and angry I could scream. But instead of lashing out, I've just made up my mind that no matter who I'm dealing with, they'll know that I'm one intelligent black person.

Racism isn't the only problem blacks have to deal with. It doesn't help that black people aren't trying to work together and build each other up. People like Harriet Tubman, Rosa Parks, and Martin Luther King Jr. literally put their lives on the line to keep us, black people, from being treated like animals. And look at what we've given them in return: black-on-black crime, black drug dealers, and black gang members.

It seems like young black men think that if they're not getting anywhere in life, you shouldn't either.

When I was younger, I used to see my dad and his friends on the corner drinking beer all night. Or I'd watch how they would pretend to give each other handshakes, when they were just trading drugs and money. I didn't want to be a part of my dad's life then, because to me it was a total embarrassment. Things like that make all black men look bad.

I think young blacks need positive black people to look up to. We need people who will encourage us to strive for the best. We don't need people telling us that everything is the white man's fault, or rapping about robbing banks and selling drugs. Unfortunately, it seems like black men hardly ever encourage each other to do good things. They're quick to tell you how to make some fast money, but will laugh in your face if you ask them about a good college.

I live in a group home for kids in foster care, where the majority of boys are black. At first, I thought we would all try to get along and help each other out. Not true. They give the highest praise to someone who just got in a fight or cursed out the staff. But if you're doing things like working hard in school, following the rules, and trying to better yourself, they act as if you're below their level. It seems like young black men think that if they're not getting anywhere in life, you shouldn't either. This attitude makes it hard for the blacks who are doing well—or are trying to do well—to shine.

Black people who have used their education to succeed should show off what they've got.

I think this is why some professional blacks don't want to associate themselves with their own race. They'd rather be on their own than be tied to the stereotypes about black people. And the stereotypes are all over the media. When I flip on the TV news, all I see are stories about some young black man who robbed a store or killed someone. I know these aren't the only stories out there. But because of all these negative images, people often assume that if a black man is driving an expensive car, he is a drug dealer or he stole it.

That's why black people who have used their education to succeed should show off what they've got. Show those people who think blacks can't get anywhere that we can and we have.

We are astronauts, basketball champions, actors, teachers, and even millionaires. And don't only show people of other races how far you've come—show other blacks, as well. Let the young blacks know that they can do more than hang out on the corner and sell drugs for a living. They can be somebody, and they can get what they want legally.

When I'm older and working (and driving around in a Mercedes), it's going to be my education, intelligence, and hard work that got me my nice clothes and fancy car. Everything I earn, wear, drive, say, and do will show not just that I am on top, but that I got there through hard work and education.

Norman wrote this story when he was 16.

John Morgan

A Floor for Every Race

By April Daley

Rainbows are beautiful products of nature. People admire them and describe their colors as one harmonious spectrum. Few people would describe them as individual blocks of different colors existing side by side yet separate. But if you think about it, that's what they are.

My school building is a 10-story rainbow where we exist together as Stuyvesant HS students but separate ourselves according to race and ethnicity. When I started as a freshman nearly four years ago, I quickly realized there weren't a lot of black people. On my first day, a black girl came up to me, introduced herself as a senior and invited me to come up to the 5th floor at any time. She told me that's where all the black people were. I made my way up there later in the week and found she was right.

There was a group of black and Latino kids sitting around in the hall, laughing and playing cards with the rare glance at a textbook. I learned that there were other floors just like this in the school, each filled with a different race or ethnic background, where students hung out in between classes and during their free periods. There was the 4th floor for Middle Eastern students, the 5th floor for black and Latino students, and the 6th floor for Asian students. The white students hung out on all of the other floors in separate clusters of their own, in a mix of ethnicities and religions. There were no signs labeling each floor, and no one was confined to these floors. It was a choice we all made.

The school administration didn't encourage it but they didn't exactly discourage it either. Once I even heard of someone being kicked off a floor based on race—not by a student but by an adult. On Chinese New Year last year, some Asian students stayed home to celebrate, so there were fewer Asians on the 6th floor than usual. A few black and Latino students decided to try to "take over" the 6th floor for the day because they thought it would be funny. While they were hanging out up there, a security officer came by and asked them to leave because, he said, they weren't on

Skin color is one of the first things that we notice, an obvious common ground.

"the right floor." When I heard the story from another black student, we were both outraged. Still, no one ever questioned the security guard.

I realize that people from other schools might look at our floor system and call us all racists. But I don't think it's racism. We don't use the floors as our separate victory corners where we chant one race's superiority over another. They are simply small communities.

In a school with more than 3,000 students, it's normal to want to find a place where we feel comfortable, somewhere we can find people who are somewhat like us. Skin color is one of the first things that we notice, an obvious common ground. But despite the separate floors, I've never confined myself to black friends at school. I've met people of all different races in my classes. In fact, I met one of my closest friends in my sophomore chemistry class. She's white. Most of the time we hung out at dance club after school. But sometimes she'd come find me on the 5th floor. Because she was my friend, no one gave her weird looks or said anything rude.

And since my classmates and I became seniors, we've strangely stopped going to our floors as often. Instead, we've started coming together as a class. We spend more time at the senior bar, an area on the 2nd floor where most of the seniors hang out, regardless of race.

I think we all mix together during senior year because after three years in the same school, we know and are friends with a lot more people of all different races. By our last year, everyone can hang out comfortably. Senior year we bond as a school, not separately as minority populations in a school. On the 2nd floor, seniors of all different backgrounds complete our 10-story rainbow.

April wrote this when she was 17. She went on to study journalism at Northwestern University.

Aaron Mendoza

Racism Ended Our Relationship

By Lenny Jones

Dear Maggie,

I know I'm probably the last person on earth that you want to hear from, but I'm writing you this letter to apologize for the way I treated you, to explain why I did the things I did, and to set things straight. So sit back and relax—it's going to be a long ride.

Before I met you, I remember hearing a lot about the controversy of interracial dating from my friends and on TV talk shows. On every show, there seemed to be some Afrocentric woman yelling from the crowd that black men shouldn't go outside their race, because black women have all that they would ever need. If not that, there's some white girl's mother protesting against an interracial relationship because she claims a black boyfriend

beat on her daughter. I didn't really care about all the controversy. I thought that if two people loved each other (you and I,
for instance), race didn't matter. But that was before we started
dating.

About two summers ago, when we first met at your mother's
house, I thought you were cool. You were Jewish but not that
religious. I guess that was just the way your family brought you
up. Anyway, we seemed to hit it off pretty well. As we got to
know each other better, you ended up being my first girlfriend
of a different race. I didn't see anything wrong with it. You were
just like any other girl and you pretty much acted like one, too
(that's a good thing, by the way).

The only problem was all the negative reactions from friends
and perfect strangers. They called me a sellout for going out with
"white trash." One time this old black lady saw us and called me
a "volunteer slave." The criticism bothered me a lot and it kind
of gnawed its way through our relationship.

Another problem was that I was thinking of joining the
Nation of Islam because I felt a sense of unity with my brothers
and sisters, and some of the Nation's beliefs I can agree with. (All
those other religions never really interested me.) The thought of
joining the Nation of Islam became bigger and bigger as our relationship went on. But there was one big problem—a friend told
me that the Nation prohibited interracial dating.

Because of my inability to communicate (what do you
expect—I'm a guy), our relationship kept getting weaker
and weaker. I never told you about all the problems I was dealing with. I hid my feelings and went on like nothing was wrong.

The things people were saying really started to sink into my
head. I started to ask myself, "Am I really a sellout?" and "Am I
really so desperate that I have to go out with a white girl?"

I was really self-conscious when I went out with you in public. Whenever we left your mostly white neighborhood and went

to the movies, traveled on the subway, or went to a black neighborhood, I felt like everybody was staring at me. I could imagine what they were saying to themselves: "Damn, why does he have to bring that around here?"

I was so scared of what people might say that I didn't want to be seen in public with you. Whenever we went out, you always wanted to hold hands (which I usually really liked). But when we were in a mostly black neighborhood or when a group of black people walked by, I tried to get you to let go of me with stupid excuses like, "My wrist is hurting," or, "I got arthritis," and I played it off like I didn't even know you. Then you would want to hold the other hand and I would make even stupider excuses like, "If one hand hurts, the other may too," or, "My hand fell asleep."

I know that my excuses probably bothered you a lot (although not as much as they

The more I saw you, the more I hated you because of what your ancestors did to mine.

bothered me), but you would wait a while and then ask me, "Did your hand wake up yet?" You never told me that I hurt your feelings and I never asked.

Another problem was that you lived upstate and I only saw you every other week. When you weren't around, I was hearing a lot of negative things from my Nation friends, like, "She's a devil," "Stay with your own people," and "Keep away from those white people. They're just trying to control you."

Other friends who thought they were so smart (yet always failed history class) gave me history lessons. They told me that I was disrespecting Malcolm X and his faith at the same time I was trying to join it. They also talked about how white people enslaved us for hundreds of years and how blacks lost their lives in wars so that we could be free and, in return, I was just spitting on their graves.

I thought a lot about what they were saying, Maggie, and

I began to despise you. I thought a lot more about joining the Nation. The more I saw you, the more I hated you because of what your ancestors did to mine. Everything you did annoyed me for no reason.

And the weirdest thing of all is that whenever I was at your house, you always wanted to watch Spike Lee's film about Malcolm X (your favorite movie). Here I was, trying not to let racism ruin our relationship, and there you were, watching a three-hour movie about a black nationalist leader. Watching the movie forced me to think about every negative thing that was said about our relationship. When the movie ended you'd sit there and smile, while I sat there pissed off.

What really surprised me was that your family treated me with the utmost respect. They didn't give me any strange looks or nasty comments. They treated me like one of the family and in return I feel like I stabbed them in the back. I feel ashamed.

I'm not going to let ignorance or racism destroy any future relationships.

Unfortunately, when it came to my own family, I was too paranoid and afraid to tell them that we were going out. Remember the time we went on that family picnic and I decided to bring you along? I didn't want to tell my family that we were going out. I told them we were just friends, and I made sure you didn't make any "beyond friendly" contact with me. I didn't really want to know how my family felt, since I was the first in the family (that I know of) to be in an interracial relationship.

Anyway, our relationship continued while I was practicing to join the Nation of Islam. I stopped eating pork, tried to fast for 30 days, and prayed to Allah (the Muslim God). Now it was time for me to choose between a religion that I felt comfortable with or being with someone who truly loved me.

Unfortunately, I made the wrong choice. I decided to go with the religion. I stopped taking your phone calls and wouldn't call you back. I basically stayed away from you and made up excuses. I told you I was grounded or I made you think that I thought you were cheating on me (which I knew you didn't do). During this whole ordeal, I felt my heart constantly snapping apart and I was getting depressed. I turned a beautiful experience into something horrible and distasteful. I just wanted you out of my life and didn't really care about your feelings. I regret that now.

During the time that I spent alone, without you, I was able to think about our break up and how I treated you. I was so worried about my reputation that I totally separated myself from you and everything you had to offer. We could have had a picture perfect relationship, but I had to go and screw it up.

The funny thing is that the "friends" who told me everything that was wrong with you (even though they never met you) hadn't had a monogamous relationship in who knows how long (and from the way they were going, wouldn't have one any time soon). You also made me realize how much of a follower I am and how much I need to be accepted. I never really hated you, but I let people make me believe that I should.

I feel really stupid about what I did and wish I could tell you I'm sorry face-to-face, but I know that will never happen and I have to deal with it. But if you're reading this now, I sincerely apologize for my behavior. I treated you like a nobody and I guess you got the picture because after a while you never called or wrote me again.

I was so depressed not hearing from you that I gave up the idea of joining the Nation. I realized I didn't feel comfortable not being able to date whoever I wanted to. The religion that I was about to join was trying to change me. Because of religion and society's attitudes I lost someone very special, and I will never have your heart again. I know about all the stuff done by white people in the past, but I'm not going to let ignorance or racism destroy any future relationships.

If anything, you made me open my eyes to the racism that was in me and all of us. Maggie, you shouldn't have gone through all the stuff I put you through, but what's done is done and I'm ready to learn from my mistakes.

Love (I hope),

Lenny

Lenny was 18 when he wrote this story. As a researcher for travel books, he has traveled extensively around the world.

Baudilio Lozado

All Mixed Up

By Satra Wasserman

In the fantasy game Dungeons & Dragons, players get to create their own characters. First you choose your race (Human, Elf, Dwarf...), then your class (fighter, paladin, mage...), and finally comes alignment, or moral stance. For instance, Superman would be "lawful good," Adolf Hitler, "chaotic evil." Certain combinations are not allowed, however. A white knight in shining armor (paladin) cannot be chaotic evil.

The way the game works is not so far off from everyday life. In real life people are always looking at your race and attempting to file you into certain categories. If you are black, for example, then you only have a limited number of "alignments" to choose from if you expect to fit in with a group. Either you can wear khakis and Tommy Hilfiger shirts, go to church on Sunday, and play ball in a league, or you can walk around in baggy jeans and a hooded sweatshirt, listen to rap religiously, and smoke weed all the time.

I'm black—or at least that's what most people think when they see me—but I never fit into any of society's categories. One reason is that I'm really mixed. My mother is a southern black woman, but my father is a Jewish guy originally from New Jersey.

I was born in Manhattan in a neighborhood known as Washington Heights, and for a while race wasn't an issue. I was dark, and so was everyone else. Then during 1st grade my family moved to Staten Island, New York, and I went to a private school that was practically all white. There I was taunted every day. "Look at the black cupcake!" they'd say. Or "Why are you so dark?" "What's wrong with you?" "Maybe if you took a bath, you'd be like us." It was pretty hard to cope.

The fact that I was really a blue-eyed devil in disguise meant that I shouldn't be around their son.

In the middle of 2nd grade we moved again, to Brooklyn. Whenever I met new kids I'd think, "Great, everything is cool now, but eventually I'm going to have to answer the same questions again." It started with my last name, Wasserman. People heard it and wanted to know why this black kid had a Jewish name. "Well, my dad's Jewish," I'd explain. No big deal.

Then it came time for my first parent-teacher conference. I remember walking home wishing that Mom would be the one to go. "Don't let them see my dad," I thought. If Mom went, then at least I could look normal, without the hassle. In the end Dad came, however, and I could feel the eyes on my back. The next day, everybody at school was waiting with the same questions that I'd been answering all my life. "Hey, who was that guy?" they asked.

"My dad."

"No, he's not your father. Are you adopted?"

When I told them no, they wouldn't believe me.

"No, you just don't know," they insisted. "Your parents didn't tell you." It made me so mad. Why couldn't anyone at least believe that it was possible to be mixed?

I remember another time my dad and I were standing on a corner, just talking, and an older black guy came up to me and asked if this guy was my father. He seemed to be worried, like my dad might be trying to kidnap me or something. My father and I are so close, but to this other guy we seemed to be strangers. That really bothered me.

In the middle of my 4th grade year we moved to the Bronx. By this point my parents had split up, so it was just me and Mom. One of the first friends I made in school was a skinny black kid named Dee. We used to bug out. We'd stick M-80s into payphones, light them, run away, and then collect all the quarters and go play video games.

We hung out a lot at Dee's house. He lived in the projects with his sister, brother, and his parents. Sometimes I would chill with his family, and we'd sit around the dinner table talking about the last time the Knicks played. I would bump into Dee's father at the barbershop and our mothers would see each other in the laundromat and chat every now and then. We were chillin'.

Then after about a year, things changed. Every time Dee asked his parents if I could come over, the answer was always no. When I called and asked to speak to him, his father would be like, "No, he's busy" or "No, he's not here." Once I was talking to Dee and I had to get off the phone for a few minutes. When I called back 10 minutes later, his father told me he wasn't there. I would see his parents on the street, and they would say hi but not much else. I started to realize that they just didn't want me around their son. As you can imagine, I was pretty confused. "Why are they treating me like a disease all of the sudden?" I wondered.

After this had been going on for about a month, I finally mentioned it to my mom. She said that she was talking to Dee's mom and the subject of my father had come up. According to Mom, when Dee's mother found out that he was white, she didn't have the best reaction. My mother didn't tell me exactly what she said but I understood that it wasn't good.

Finally everything was clear. Even though they had known me for months, the fact that I was really a blue-eyed devil in disguise meant that I shouldn't be around their son. Dee and I remained tight. The fact that I was mixed wasn't an issue for him, but now all of a sudden we couldn't chill like we used to.

The whole thing was pretty wack. I mean, come on, how are you going to cut someone off just because he's half white? I couldn't change the fact that I was mixed. Besides, they knew me. It's not like I was a spy on a mission to convert their son to the dark (or light) side. And to top it all off, I couldn't have been older than 10, 11 at the most. Something like that would be weird enough now, but back then it had me feeling really awkward and self-conscious.

The biggest favor I did for myself was not trying to choose one race to be.

I reached the height of my isolation in junior high school. The 8th grade was the worst nine months of my life. Because of the way I speak, I was officially knighted "Sir Oreo." Every day was an adventure. People would mess with me all the time. On top of being weird, I was small, probably around 5'4" and 110 pounds. I got pushed around and beat up. People would talk trash about my name, too. "Yo Satra, is that a girl's name?" "I got a dog named Sasha." I had to listen to this all the time.

It was beyond being different; I was an alien who lived completely in my own world of baseball, video games, and my comic book collection. My only connections to the world around me were dodgeball and handball, and Street Fighter (and I don't care how nice you are, I'll whip your ass!). The latest fashions and walking "left foot first" meant nothing to me. But in the minds of my 12- and 13-year-old classmates, this was mad important. I was always the weirdo.

The biggest favor I did for myself was not trying to choose one race to be, which is a mistake most people in my situation make. The reason is that if I decided I was going to be black, first I'd have to figure out what that meant. I'd be watching other people and imitating their image. Or, even worse, I would be watching TV or listening to music, trying to imitate the media's idea of blackness. And the same thing went for trying to be white. OK, first I'd have to dress like this, then I'd have to talk like that, then I'd have to walk like so and hang out with those guys over there. It goes on and on.

I have often wondered why I am the way I am at this point. Looking back at my life has given me an answer. When I was younger, white kids in school would bother me for being so dark. Later on, black kids would ask what was wrong with me because I was so light. Finally, I realized you just can't please everybody. Now I just do my own thing. Wake up, put on some old school hip-hop, then go out to play handball. I dress, talk, look, say, and do what I want, the way I want.

To this day there is really no one particular group that I'm down with, but on the other hand I have so many hobbies that I can chill with all kinds of different people. My relationships are based on interests. Some people I meet through rap, just standing around freestyling. Others I meet on the handball court. Right now this system is working out nicely. It feels like I'm rebelling against the demons of my past by just being myself.

Satra wrote this story when he was 17. He later completed high school and went on to college.

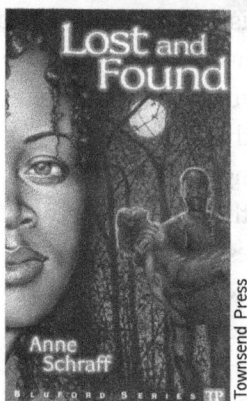

Lost and Found

Darcy Wills winced at the loud rap music coming from her sister's room.

My rhymes were rockin'
MC's were droppin'
People shoutin' and hip-hoppin'
Step to me and you'll be inferior
'Cause I'm your lyrical superior.

Darcy went to Grandma's room. The darkened room smelled of lilac perfume, Grandma's favorite, but since her stroke Grandma did not notice it, or much of anything.

"Bye, Grandma," Darcy whispered from the doorway. "I'm going to school now."

Just then, the music from Jamee's room cut off, and Jamee rushed into the hallway.

The teen characters in the Bluford novels, a fiction series by Townsend Press, struggle with many of the same difficult issues that our students write about. Here's the first chapter from *Lost and Found*, by Anne Schraff, the first book in the series. In this novel, high school sophomore Darcy contends with the return of her long-absent father, the troubling behavior of her younger sister Jamee, and the beginning of her first relationship.

"Like she even hears you," Jamee said as she passed Darcy. Just two years younger than Darcy, Jamee was in eighth grade, though she looked older.

"It's still nice to talk to her. Sometimes she understands. You want to pretend she's not here or something?"

"She's not," Jamee said, grabbing her backpack.

"Did you study for your math test?" Darcy asked. Mom was an emergency room nurse who worked rotating shifts. Most of the time, Mom was too tired to pay much attention to the girls' schoolwork. So Darcy tried to keep track of Jamee.

"Mind your own business," Jamee snapped.

"You got two D's on your last report card," Darcy scolded. "You wanna flunk?" Darcy did not want to sound like a nagging parent, but Jamee wasn't doing her best. Maybe she couldn't make A's like Darcy, but she could do better.

Jamee stomped out of the apartment, slamming the door behind her. "Mom's trying to get some rest!" Darcy yelled. "Do you have to be so selfish?" But Jamee was already gone, and the apartment was suddenly quiet.

Darcy loved her sister. Once, they had been good friends. But now all Jamee cared about was her new group of rowdy friends. They leaned on cars outside of school and turned up rap music on their boom boxes until the street seemed to tremble like an earthquake. Jamee had even stopped hanging out with her old friend Alisha Wrobel, something she used to do every weekend.

Darcy went back into the living room, where her mother sat in the recliner sipping coffee. "I'll be home at 2:30, Mom," Darcy said. Mom smiled faintly. She was tired, always tired. And lately she was worried too. The hospital where she worked was cutting staff. It seemed each day fewer people were expected to do more work. It was like trying to climb a mountain that keeps getting taller as you go. Mom was forty-four, but just yesterday she said, "I'm like an old car that's run out of warranty, baby. You know what happens then. Old car is ready for the junk heap. Well, maybe that hospital is gonna tell me one of these days—'Mattie Mae Wills, we don't need you anymore. We can get somebody younger and cheaper.'"

"Mom, you're not old at all," Darcy had said, but they were only words, empty words. They could not erase the dark, weary lines from beneath her mother's eyes.

Darcy headed down the street toward Bluford High School. It was not a terrible neighborhood they lived in; it just was not good. Many front yards were not cared for. Debris—fast food wrappers, plastic bags, old newspapers—blew around and piled against fences and curbs. Darcy hated that. Sometimes she and other kids from school spent Saturday mornings cleaning up, but it seemed a losing battle. Now, as she walked, she tried to focus on small spots of beauty along the way. Mrs. Walker's pink and white roses bobbed proudly in the morning breeze. The Hustons' rock garden was carefully designed around a wooden windmill.

As she neared Bluford, Darcy thought about the science project that her biology teacher, Ms. Reed, was assigning. Darcy was doing hers on tidal pools. She was looking forward to visiting a real tidal pool, taking pictures, and doing research. Today, Ms. Reed would be dividing the students into teams of two. Darcy wanted to be paired with her close friend, Brisana Meeks. They were both excellent students, a cut above most kids at Bluford, Darcy thought.

"Today, we are forming project teams so that each student can gain something valuable from the other," Ms. Reed said as Darcy sat at her desk. Ms. Reed was a tall, stately woman who reminded Darcy of the Statue of Liberty. She would have been a perfect model for the statue if Lady Liberty had been a black woman. She never would have been called pretty, but it was possible she might have been called a handsome woman. "For this assignment, each of you will be working with someone you've never worked with before."

Darcy was worried. If she was not teamed with Brisana,

maybe she would be teamed with some really dumb student who would pull her down. Darcy was a little ashamed of herself for thinking that way. Grandma used to say that all flowers are equal, but different. The simple daisy was just as lovely as the prize rose. But still Darcy did not want to be paired with some weak partner who would lower her grade.

"Darcy Wills will be teamed with Tarah Carson," Ms. Reed announced.

Darcy gasped. Not Tarah! Not that big, chunky girl with the brassy voice who squeezed herself into tight skirts and wore lime green or hot pink satin tops and cheap jewelry. Not Tarah who hung out with Cooper Hodden, that loser who was barely hanging on to his football eligibility. Darcy had heard that Cooper had been left back once or twice and even got his driver's license as a sophomore. Darcy's face felt hot with anger. Why was Ms. Reed doing this?

Hakeem Randall, a handsome, shy boy who sat in the back row, was teamed with the class blabbermouth, LaShawn Appleby. Darcy had a secret crush on Hakeem since freshman year. So far she had only shared this with her diary, never with another living soul.

It was almost as though Ms. Reed was playing some devilish game. Darcy glanced at Tarah, who was smiling broadly. Tarah had an enormous smile, and her teeth contrasted harshly with her dark red lipstick. "Great," Darcy muttered under her breath.

Ms. Reed ordered the teams to meet so they could begin to plan their projects.

As she sat down by Tarah, Darcy was instantly sickened by a syrupy-sweet odor.

She must have doused herself with cheap perfume this morning, Darcy thought.

"Hey, girl," Tarah said. "Well, don't you look down in the mouth. What's got you lookin' that way?"

It was hard for Darcy to meet new people, especially someone like Tarah, a person Aunt Charlotte would call "low class." These were people who were loud and rude. They drank too much, used drugs, got into fights and ruined the neighborhood. They yelled ugly insults at people, even at their friends. Darcy did not actually know that Tarah did anything like this personally, but she seemed like the type who did.

"I just didn't think you'd be interested in tidal pools," Darcy explained.

Tarah slammed her big hand on the desk, making her gold bracelets jangle like ice cubes in a glass, and laughed. Darcy had never heard a mule bray, but she was sure it made exactly the same sound. Then Tarah leaned close and whispered, "Girl, I don't know a tidal pool from a fool. Ms. Reed stuck us together to mess with our heads, you hear what I'm sayin'?"

"Maybe we could switch to other partners," Darcy said nervously.

A big smile spread slowly over Tarah's face. "Nah, I think I'm gonna enjoy this. You're always sittin' here like a princess collecting your A's. Now you gotta work with a regular person, so you better loosen up, girl!"

Darcy felt as if her teeth were glued to her tongue. She fumbled in her bag for her outline of the project. It all seemed like a horrible joke now. She and Tarah Carson standing knee-deep in the muck of a tidal pool!

"Worms live there, don't they?" Tarah asked, twisting a big gold ring on her chubby finger.

"Yeah, I guess," Darcy replied.

"Big green worms," Tarah continued. "So if you get your feet stuck in the bottom of that old tidal pool, and you can't get out, do the worms crawl up your clothes?"

Darcy ignored the remark. "I'd like for us to go there soon, you know, look around."

"My boyfriend, Cooper, he goes down to the ocean all the time. He can take us. He says he's seen these fiddler crabs. They look like big spiders, and they'll try to bite your toes off. Cooper says so," Tarah said.

"Stop being silly," Darcy shot back. "If you' re not even going to be serious . . . "

"You think you're better than me, don't you?" Tarah suddenly growled.

"I never said—" Darcy blurted.

"You don't have to say it, girl. It's in your eyes. You think I'm a low-life and you're something special. Well, I got more friends than you got fingers and toes together. You got no friends, and everybody laughs at you behind your back. Know what the word on you is? Darcy Wills give you the chills."

Just then, the bell rang, and Darcy was glad for the excuse to turn away from Tarah, to hide the hot tears welling in her eyes. She quickly rushed from the classroom, relieved that school was over. Darcy did not think she could bear to sit through another class just now.

Darcy headed down the long street towards home. She did not like Tarah. Maybe it was wrong, but it was true. Still, Tarah's brutal words hurt. Even stupid, awful people might tell you the truth about yourself. And Darcy did not have any real friends, except for Brisana. Maybe the other kids were mocking her behind her back. Darcy was very slender, not as shapely as many of the other girls. She remembered the time when Cooper Hodden was hanging in front of the deli with his friends, and he yelled as Darcy went by, "Hey, is that really a female there? Sure don't look like it. Looks more like an old broomstick with hair." His companions laughed rudely, and Darcy had walked a little faster.

A terrible thought clawed at Darcy. Maybe she was the loser, not Tarah. Tarah was always hanging with a bunch of kids, laughing and joking. She would go down the hall to the lockers and greetings would come from everywhere. "Hey, Tarah!" "What's up, Tar?" "See ya at lunch, girl." When Darcy went to the lockers, there was dead silence.

Darcy usually glanced into stores on her way home from school. She enjoyed looking at the trays of chicken feet and pork ears at the little Asian grocery store. Sometimes she would even steal a glance at the diners sitting by the picture window at the Golden Grill Restaurant. But today she stared straight ahead, her shoulders drooping.

If this had happened last year, she would have gone directly to Grandma's house, a block from where Darcy lived. How many times had Darcy and Jamee run to Grandma's, eaten applesauce cookies, drunk cider, and poured out their troubles to Grandma. Somehow, their problems would always dissolve in the warmth of her love and wisdom. But now Grandma was a frail figure in the corner of their apartment, saying little. And what little she did say made less and less sense.

Darcy was usually the first one home. The minute she got there, Mom left for the hospital to take the 3:00 to 11:00 shift in the ER. By the time Mom finished her paperwork at the hospital, she would be lucky to be home again by midnight. After Mom left, Darcy went to Grandma's room to give her the malted nutrition drink that the doctor ordered her to have three times a day.

"Want to drink your chocolate malt, Grandma?" Darcy asked, pulling up a chair beside Grandma's bed.

Grandma was sitting up, and her eyes were open. "No. I'm not hungry," she said listlessly. She always said that.

"You need to drink your malt, Grandma," Darcy insisted, gently putting the straw between the pinched lips.

Grandma sucked the malt slowly. "Grandma, nobody likes me at school," Darcy said. She did not expect any response. But there was a strange comfort in telling Grandma anyway. "Everybody laughs at me. It's because I'm shy and maybe stuck-up, too, I guess. But I don't mean to be. Stuck-up, I mean. Maybe I'm weird. I could be weird, I guess. I could be like Aunt Charlotte . . ." Tears rolled down Darcy's cheeks. Her heart ached with loneliness. There was nobody to talk to anymore, nobody who had time to listen, nobody who understood.

Grandma blinked and pushed the straw away. Her eyes brightened as they did now and then. "You are a wonderful girl. Everybody knows that," Grandma said in an almost normal voice. It happened like that sometimes. It was like being in the middle of a dark storm and having the clouds part, revealing a patch of clear, sunlit blue. For just a few precious minutes, Grandma was bright-eyed and saying normal things.

"Oh, Grandma, I'm so lonely," Darcy cried, pressing her head against Grandma's small shoulder.

"You were such a beautiful baby," Grandma said, stroking her hair. "'That one is going to shine like the morning star.' That's what I told your Mama. 'That child is going to shine like the morning star.' Tell me, Angelcake, is your daddy home yet?"

Darcy straightened. "Not yet." Her heart pounded so hard, she could feel it thumping in her chest. Darcy's father had not been home in five years.

"Well, tell him to see me when he gets home. I want him to buy you that blue dress you liked in the store window. That's for you, Angelcake. Tell him I've got money. My social security came, you know. I have money for the blue dress," Grandma said, her eyes slipping shut.

Just then, Darcy heard the apartment door slam. Jamee had come home. Now she stood in the hall, her hands belligerently on her hips. "Are you talking to Grandma again?" Jamee demanded.

"She was talking like normal," Darcy said. "Sometimes she does. You know she does."

"That is so stupid," Jamee snapped. "She never says anything right anymore. Not anything!" Jamee's voice trembled.

Darcy got up quickly and set down the can of malted milk. She ran to Jamee and put her arms around her sister. "Jamee, I know you're hurting too."

"Oh, don't be stupid," Jamee protested, but Darcy hugged her more tightly, and in a few seconds Jamee was crying. "She was the best thing in this stupid house," Jamee cried. "Why'd she have to go?"

"She didn't go," Darcy said. "Not really."

"She did! She did!" Jamee sobbed. She struggled free of Darcy, ran to her room, and slammed the door. In a minute, Darcy heard the bone-rattling sound of rap music.

Lost and Found, a Bluford Series™ novel, is reprinted with permission from Townsend Press. Copyright © 2002.

Want to read more? This and other Bluford Series™ novels and paperbacks can be purchased for $1 each at www.townsendpress.com.

Teens:
How to Get More Out of This Book

Self-help: The teens who wrote the stories in this book did so because they hope that telling their stories will help readers who are facing similar challenges. They want you to know that you are not alone, and that taking specific steps can help you manage or overcome very difficult situations. They've done their best to be clear about the actions that worked for them so you can see if they'll work for you.

Writing: You can also use the book to improve your writing skills. Each teen in this book wrote 5-10 drafts of his or her story before it was published. If you read the stories closely you'll see that the teens work to include a beginning, a middle, and an end, and good scenes, description, dialogue, and anecdotes (little stories). To improve your writing, take a look at how these writers construct their stories. Try some of their techniques in your own writing.

Reading: Finally, you'll notice that we include the first chapter from a Bluford Series novel in this book, alongside the true stories by teens. We hope you'll like it enough to continue reading. The more you read, the more you'll strengthen your reading skills. Teens at Youth Communication like the Bluford novels because they explore themes similar to those in their own stories. Your school may already have the Bluford books. If not, you can order them online for only $1.

Resources on the Web

We will occasionally post Think About It questions on our website, www.youthcomm.org, to accompany stories in this and other Youth Communication books. We try out the questions with teens and post the ones they like best. Many teens report that writing answers to those questions in a journal is very helpful.

How to Use This Book in Staff Training

Staff say that reading these stories gives them greater insight into what teens are thinking and feeling, and new strategies for working with them. You can help the staff you work with by using these stories as case studies.

Select one story to read in the group, and ask staff to identify and discuss the main issue facing the teen. There may be disagreement about this, based on the background and experience of staff. That is fine. One point of the exercise is that teens have complex lives and needs. Adults can probably be more effective if they don't focus too narrowly and can see several dimensions of their clients.

Ask staff: What issues or feelings does the story provoke in them? What kind of help do they think the teen wants? What interventions are likely to be most promising? Least effective? Why? How would you build trust with the teen writer? How have other adults failed the teen, and how might that affect his or her willingness to accept help? What other resources would be helpful to this teen, such as peer support, a mentor, counseling, family therapy, etc?

Resources on the Web

From time to time we will post Think About It questions on our website, www.youthcomm.org, to accompany stories in this and other Youth Communication books. We try out the questions with teens and post the ones that they find most effective. We'll also post lessons for some of the stories. Adults can use the questions and lessons in workshops.

Discussion Guide

Teachers and Staff:
How to Use This Book in Groups

When working with teens individually or in groups, you can use these stories to help young people face difficult issues in a way that feels safe to them. That's because talking about the issues in the stories usually feels safer to teens than talking about those same issues in their own lives. Addressing issues through the stories allows for some personal distance; they hit close to home, but not too close. Talking about them opens up a safe place for reflection. As teens gain confidence talking about the issues in the stories, they usually become more comfortable talking about those issues in their own lives.

Below are general questions to guide your discussion. In most cases you can read a story and conduct a discussion in one 45-minute session. Teens are usually happy to read the stories aloud, with each teen reading a paragraph or two. (Allow teens to pass if they don't want to read.) It takes 10-15 minutes to read a story straight through. However, it is often more effective to let workshop participants make comments and discuss the story as you go along. The workshop leader may even want to annotate her copy of the story beforehand with key questions.

If teens read the story ahead of time or silently, it's good to break the ice with a few questions that get everyone on the same page: Who is the main character? How old is she? What happened to her? How did she respond? Another good starting question is: "What stood out for you in the story?" Go around the room and let each person briefly mention one thing.

Then move on to open-ended questions, which encourage participants to think more deeply about what the writers were feeling, the choices they faced, and the actions they took. There are no right or wrong answers to the open-ended questions.

Open-ended questions encourage participants to think about how the themes, emotions, and choices in the stories relate to their own lives. Here are some examples of open-ended questions that we have found to be effective. You can use variations of these questions with almost any story in this book.

—What main problem or challenge did the writer face?

—What choices did the teen have in trying to deal with the problem?

—Which way of dealing with the problem was most effective for the teen? Why?

—What strengths, skills, or resources did the teen use to address the challenge?

—If you were in the writer's shoes, what would you have done?

—What could adults have done better to help this young person?

—What have you learned by reading this story that you didn't know before?

—What, if anything, will you do differently after reading this story?

—What surprised you in this story?

—Do you have a different view of this issue, or see a different way of dealing with it, after reading this story? Why or why not?

Credits

The stories in this book originally appeared in the following Youth Communication publications:

"How the Other Half Lives," by Natasha Santos, *New Youth Connections*, December 2005; "Not Black Enough?" by Jamal Greene, *New Youth Connections*, September/October 1994; "I'm Black, He's Puerto Rican. So What?" by Artiqua Steed, *New Youth Connections*, January/February 1996; "Shopping While Black," by Stephanie Hinkson, *New Youth Connections*, April 2005; "Rappin' with the 5-0," by Allen Francis, *New Youth Connections*, November 1993; "Princess Oreo Speaks Out," by Dwan "Telly" Carter, *New Youth Connections*, March 2001; "Lightening My Skin, Straightening My Hair," by Samantha Brown, *New Youth Connections*, September/October 1997; "The Whitest Black Girl," by Nicole Hawkins, *New Youth Connections*, January/February 1999; "Barack Is Black," by April Daley, *New Youth Connections*, May/June 2007; "Barack Is Black...But Not African-American," by Donald Moore, *New Youth Connections*, May/June 2007; "Don't Follow the Leader," by Anonymous, *Represent*, March/April 2006; "Big, Black, and Beautiful," by Anonymous, *New Youth Connections*, December 1997; "The N-Word," by Desiree Bailey, *New Youth Connections*, May/June 2007; "Singled Out," by Angelina Darrisaw, *New Youth Connections*, September/October 2002; "The Flag's Not for Me," by Anonymous, *New Youth Connections*, November 2001; "Where My Girls At?" by Danielle Chambers, *Represent*, Fall 2009; "My First White Friend," by Anita Ames, *New Youth Connections*, May/June 2007; "Black Girl, White Campus," by Samantha Brown, *New Youth Connections*, November 1998; "Coloring Outside the Lines," by Desiree Bailey, *New Youth Connections*, March 2006; "Black Pride, and a New Ride," by Norman Brant, *Represent*, July/August 1998; "A Floor for Every Race," by April Daley, *New Youth Connections*, May/June 2007; "Racism Ended Our Relationship," by Lenny Jones, *Represent*, July/August 1997; "All Mixed Up," by Satra Wasserman, *New Youth Connections*, April 1997.

About
Youth Communication

Youth Communication, founded in 1980, is a nonprofit youth development program located in New York City whose mission is to teach writing, journalism, and leadership skills. The teenagers we train become writers for our websites and books and for two print magazines: *New Youth Connections*, a general-interest youth magazine, and *Represent*, a magazine by and for young people in foster care.

Each year, up to 100 young people participate in Youth Communication's after school and summer journalism workshops, where they work under the direction of full-time professional editors. Most are African-American, Latino, or Asian, and many are recent immigrants. The opportunity to reach their peers with accurate portrayals of their lives and important self-help information motivates the young writers to create powerful stories.

Our goal is to run a strong youth development program in which teens produce high quality stories that inform and inspire their peers. Doing so requires us to be sensitive to the complicated lives and emotions of the teen participants while also providing an intellectually rigorous experience. We achieve that goal in the writing/teaching/editing relationship, which is the core of our program.

Our teaching and editorial process begins with discussions

between adult editors and the teen staff. In those meetings, the teens and the editors work together to identify the most important issues in the teens' lives and to figure out how those issues can be turned into stories that will resonate with teen readers.

Once story topics are chosen, students begin the process of crafting their stories. For a personal story, that means revisiting events in one's past to understand their significance for the future. For a commentary, it means developing a logical and persuasive point of view. For a reported story, it means gathering information through research and interviews. Students look inward and outward as they try to make sense of their experiences and the world around them and find the points of intersection between personal and social concerns. That process can take a few weeks or a few months. Stories frequently go through 10 or more drafts as students work under the guidance of their editors, the way any professional writer does.

Many of the students who walk through our doors have uneven skills, as a result of poor education, living under extremely stressful conditions, or coming from homes where English is a second language. Yet, to complete their stories, students must successfully perform a wide range of activities, including writing and rewriting, reading, discussion, reflection, research, interviewing, and typing. They must work as members of a team and they must accept individual responsibility. They learn to provide constructive criticism, and to accept it. They engage in explorations of truthfulness, fairness, and accuracy. They meet deadlines. They must develop the audacity to believe that they have something important to say and the humility to recognize that saying it well is not a process of instant gratification. Rather, it usually requires a long, hard struggle through many discussions and much rewriting.

It would be impossible to teach these skills and dispositions as separate, disconnected topics, like grammar, ethics, or assertiveness. However, we find that students make rapid progress when they are learning skills in the context of an inquiry that is personally significant to them and that will benefit their peers.

When teens publish their stories—in *New Youth Connections* and *Represent,* on the Web, and in other publications—they reach tens of thousands of teen and adult readers. Teachers, counselors, social workers, and other adults circulate the stories to young people in their classes and out-of-school youth programs. Adults tell us that teens in their programs—including many who are ordinarily resistant to reading—clamor for the stories. Teen readers report that the stories give them information they can't get anywhere else, and inspire them to reflect on their lives and open lines of communication with adults.

Writers usually participate in our program for one semester, though some stay much longer. Years later, many of them report that working here was a turning point in their lives—that it helped them acquire the confidence and skills that they needed for success in college and careers. Scores of our graduates have overcome tremendous obstacles to become journalists, writers, and novelists. They include National Book Award finalist and MacArthur Fellowship winner Edwidge Danticat, novelist Ernesto Quiñonez, writer Veronica Chambers, and *New York Times* reporter Rachel Swarns. Hundreds more are working in law, business, and other careers. Many are teachers, principals, and youth workers, and several have started nonprofit youth programs themselves and work as mentors—helping another generation of young people develop their skills and find their voices.

Youth Communication is a nonprofit educational corporation. Contributions are gratefully accepted and are tax deductible to the fullest extent of the law.

To make a contribution, or for information about our publications and programs, including our catalog of over 100 books and curricula for hard-to-reach teens, see www.youthcomm.org.

About the Editors

Maria Luisa Tucker is the associate editor of *New Youth Connections*, Youth Communication's magazine by and for New York City teens. Before coming to Youth Communication, she worked as a reporter for the *Village Voice*. She has also written for several other publications, including *AlterNet.org*, an online magazine, and the *Santa Fe Reporter*, a weekly newspaper where her work garnered several awards for investigative and media reporting. She holds a bachelor's degree in journalism from Texas State University and a master's in American Studies from Columbia University.

Keith Hefner co-founded Youth Communication in 1980 and has directed it ever since. He is the recipient of the Luther P. Jackson Education Award from the New York Association of Black Journalists and a MacArthur Fellowship. He was also a Revson Fellow at Columbia University.

Laura Longhine is the editorial director at Youth Communication. She edited *Represent*, Youth Communication's magazine by and for youth in foster care, for three years, and has written for a variety of publications. She has a BA in English from Tufts University and an MS in Journalism from Columbia University.

More Helpful Books
From Youth Communication

Real Men: Urban Teens Write About How to Be a Man. What does it take to be a man? These true stories will encourage young men to recognize their strengths, improve their skills and overcome challenges to success. (Youth Communication)

Real Stories, Real Teens. Inspire teens to read and recognize their strengths with this collection of 26 true stories by teens. The young writers describe how they overcame significant challenges and stayed true to themselves. Also includes the first chapters from three novels in the Bluford Series. (Youth Communication)

Real Jobs, Real Stories. Help teens to prepare for, find, and succeed at work with these true teen-written stories about job experiences. (Youth Communication)

The Courage to Be Yourself: True Stories by Teens About Cliques, Conflicts, and Overcoming Peer Pressure. In 26 first-person stories, teens write about their lives with searing honesty. These stories will inspire young readers to reflect on their own lives, work through their problems, and help them discover who they really are. (Free Spirit)

Starting With "I": Personal Stories by Teenagers. "Who am I and who do I want to become?" Thirty-five stories examine this question through the lens of race, ethnicity, gender, sexuality, family, and more. Increase this book's value with the free Teacher's Guide, available from youthcomm.org. (Youth Communication)

The Struggle to Be Strong: True Stories by Teens About Overcoming Tough Times. Foreword by Veronica Chambers. Help young people identify and build on their own strengths with 30 personal stories about resiliency. (Free Spirit)

Out With It: Gay and Straight Teens Write About Homosexuality. Break stereotypes and provide support with this unflinching look at gay life from a teen's perspective. With a focus on urban youth, this book also includes several heterosexual teens' transformative experiences with gay peers. (Youth Communication)

Things Get Hectic: Teens Write About the Violence That Surrounds Them. Violence is commonplace in many teens' lives, be it bullying, gangs, dating, or family relationships. Hear the experiences of victims, perpetrators, and witnesses through more than 50 real-world stories. (Youth Communication)

From Dropout to Achiever: Teens Write About School. Help teens overcome the challenges of graduating, which may involve overcoming family problems, bouncing back from a bad semester, or even dropping out for a time. These teens show how they achieve academic success. (Youth Communication)

My Secret Addiction: Teens Write About Cutting. These true accounts of cutting, or self-mutilation, offer a window into the personal and family situations that lead to this secret habit, and show how teens can get the help they need. (Youth Communication)

Sticks and Stones: Teens Write About Bullying. Shed light on bullying, with stories told from the perspectives of the bully, the victim, and the witness. These stories show why bullying occurs, the harm it causes, and how it might be prevented. (Youth Communication)

To order these and other books, go to:
www.youthcomm.org
or call 212-279-0708 x115

139

www.ingramcontent.com/pod-product-compliance
Lightning Source LLC
Chambersburg PA
CBHW052210270326
41931CB00011B/2290